JOKES FOR THOSE
WHO WANT TO GIVE
AT THE OFFICE.

EMPLOYER: (to newly hired secretary): Now, I hope you understand the importance of punctuation.
SECRETARY: Oh, yes indeed, sir, I always get to work on time.

"Is your son a good executive?" asked Spivak. "My boy is so dedicated to his work," said Weber, "that he keeps his secretary near his bed in case he gets an idea during the night!"

MEDICAL NEWS UPDATE
Surgeons successfully transplanted a shark's heart into a businessman's body. The patient has fully recovered and is now a Senior Partner in a major Chicago law firm.

THE
LARRY
WILDE
LIBRARY OF
LAUGHTER

IVY BOOKS • NEW YORK

Ivy Books
Published by Ballantine Books
Copyright © 1988 by Larry Wilde

Library of Congress Catalog Card Number: 87-33887

ISBN 0-8041-1096-4

This edition published by arrangement with Jester Press

Manufactured in the United States of America

First Ballantine Books Edition: August 1993

To the beloved memory
of George Jessel
Toastmaster General of the United States

With special thanks to
Lisa Kay Reed, Jane Jordan Browne
and Maryruth Wilde.

CONTENTS

The Art of Storytelling

Most people are not born with the ability to tell stories well. Like any worthwhile skill, the ability to squeeze the last bit of laughter from a droll tale must be learned, practiced and honed to perfection.

Suppose you're a person who is too frightened to tell a joke. You forget the punchline or, worse, the entire joke. Perhaps you're someone who likes to tell stories but feels your material doesn't get the big laugh it deserves.

In the following pages we'll focus on some tried and true methods for mastering this venerable and delightful form of verbal relaxation.

Reciting tales for diversion and amusement is an ancient tradition. For centuries it was the principal form of entertainment. Kings and clergy, slaves and masters, pioneers and cowboys gathered beside fires on frosty nights and whiled away the hours listening to myths, fables and folktales.

Some fireside narrators were more gifted than others. People were hypnotically drawn to the most captivating of those tellers of tales. Folks have always loved a well-told story. And, if the storyteller had the rare qualities necessary to evoke laughter, that person was applauded, and much sought after as a social companion.

In mid-nineteenth century America three humorists came along who would turn storytelling into an honorable and profitable profession. Mark Twain, Josh Billings and Artemus Ward were master raconteurs who began their careers by producing humorous articles for newspapers and magazines and eventually published highly successful books.

But all achieved international fame on the lecture platform. It was through this medium that each man delivered his own brand of humor with material he had written for himself.

From these beginnings evolved the vaudeville jesters who specialized in doing monologues and funny stories. Among those early stars were Frank Fay, Lou Holtz and George Jessel. In later years, Danny Thomas and Myron Cohen carried on the tradition.

Today fireside frivolity has been replaced by the coffee break and the cocktail party as a social gathering place. But social storytellers remain as popular as ever.

Unfortunately, good storytellers are rare. The best of jokes can be ruined by poor delivery, unnecessary verbiage and a lack of training or experience.

It need not be that way. Good storytelling can be accomplished with practice and knowledge. Of course, knowing **how** to tell a joke is the key. The fundamental techniques can be learned.

An understanding of delivery, timing, gesture and a careful selection of material are all basic tools of the skilled tale teller. The raising of an eyebrow, a movement of the hand or a pause can help a story get a bigger laugh.

However, before getting into the **how to's** of effective story telling, it's essential to discuss the most common forms of verbal humor—anecdotes, riddles, one-line gags, jokes and stories.

An **anecdote** is a short account of a true or seemingly true incident that is interesting or amusing.

Almost everyone tells anecdotes. "What happened when I bought my new car," "How I met my spouse," "The day the water heater broke down," etc. These events are recounted over and over to friends and family. Sometimes they are humorous but rarely hilarious. It requires a uniquely skilled storyteller to take an event that at best is only mildly amusing and turn it into an uproarious account.

The humor is more effective when an anecdote is written for a reader rather than told to a listener. Stories of this sort are found in abundance in magazines like the *New Yorker*, *Punch*, and *Saturday Review*. The short stories of S.J. Perelman, Dorothy Parker, James Thurber, E.B. White and Robert Benchley are excellent examples of turning simple incidents into very funny situations.

Anecdotes told in social situations can be expected to produce smiles or at most chuckles. It is much easier to stimulate laughter with what has been categorized as the **riddle**.

A **riddle** is a perplexing or puzzling question posed as a problem to be solved or guessed, often played as a game to evoke laughter.

Children love riddles. It gives them an opportunity to ask a question and then provide a funny answer. This, of course, allows them to feel superior to the individual unable to supply the punchline.

What did the bald man say when he got a comb for his birthday?

"Thanks very much. I'll never part with it."

What did the doughnut say to the cake?
"If I had as much dough as you have, I wouldn't be hanging around this hole!"

What is the best thing to take when you're run down?
The license number of the car that hit you.

Adults might consider these silly or corny but riddles also have their place in the adult repertoire.

What is a committee?
A life form with six or more legs and no brains.

In what way does a lawyer resemble a pelican?
In the length of his bill.

What do they call a 1956 Buick in Alabama?
The bridal suite.

In show business, a funny comment or idea usually expressed in one sentence is referred to as a **one-liner**. The term encompasses quips, quotes, gaglines and comic definitions. It is perhaps the quintessential form of verbal humor, for the complete thought is expressed in a few words.

Certain comedians, such as Bob Hope, Milton Berle, specialize in one-liners, and almost all comics rely on them. Here are some classics from Henny Youngman:

Take my wife, please!

I take my wife everywhere but she always finds her way home.

Valentine's Day she gave me the usual gift— she ate my heart out.

These are from the pen of Woody Allen:

I don't believe in after-life, although I am bringing along a change of underwear.

I failed to make the chess team on account of my height.

A stockbroker is someone who invests other people's money until it's all gone.

And, of course, the wonderful wit of Will Rogers:

With Congress, every time they make a joke it's a law. And every time they make a law it's a joke.

I might have gone to West Point but I was too proud to talk to a congressman.

A bunch of American tourists were hissed and stoned in France, but not until they had finished buying.

The craft of creating one-liners is a highly respected trade in Hollywood, and creators of verbal wit are in great demand.

Perhaps the most popular form of comedic expression is the **joke**. A masterful definition is offered by Evan Esar, the esteemed humor historian, in his *The Humor of Humor*:

The **joke** is a "brief single incident, a comic tale stripped of all nonessential details. It begins with a situation, has no middle, and ends with a surprising or unexpected outcome."

Here are some samples:

> After his examination Bigelow said to the doctor, "Tell me the truth! Am I going to get well?"
>
> "Of course you are!" said the physician. "You're going to get well if it costs every cent you've got."

> Two elderly women met in the basement laundry room of their Brooklyn apartment building. "Did you hear what's happening in the Middle East?" asked one woman.
>
> "Oh, I live in the back. I don't hear anything," replied the other woman.

> A little boy walked up to his grandfather and said, "Gee, grandpa, you sure got a lot of whiskers. Can you spit through them all?"
>
> "Yes, sonny, I can."
>
> "Well, you better do it now, cause they're on fire from your pipe."

Finally, we come to the **story**:

A **story** has the same basic elements as the joke except that it is longer and has a beginning, middle and end.

Beale was getting a shave and manicure. He noticed that the pretty blonde doing his nails filled out her uniform perfectly.

"Listen, when you finish tonight," suggested Beale, "how 'bout you and me going to dinner, then the theatre, have a couple of drinks, we'll go back to my place and live it up."

"I can't," said the manicurist. "I'm married."

"Why don't you just tell your husband you're gonna stay overnight with a girlfriend."

"Why don't you? He's shaving you!"

Brad joined the paratroops and after three months of training he was up in a plane ready to make his first jump, scared to death.

"Nothing to worry about," said the sergeant. "Just count to ten and pull the cord. When you get to the ground there'll be a truck there to take you back to camp."

Brad jumped, counted to ten, pulled the rip cord but the parachute didn't open. He pulled it again. No luck. He yanked on the emergency chute. That didn't open.

"How do you like that?" mused Brad. "I bet when I get down to the ground the darn truck won't be there either."

Rafferty and his wife were sitting at a bar. She was nursing a ginger ale while he was putting away one shot of bourbon after another. "When are you gonna stop all this drinking?" complained Mrs. Rafferty.

"Oh, darlin', if you'd only try some you'd love it."

Rafferty convinced her to take a shot of straight whiskey. She sputtered and choked and coughed and finally gasped, "This stuff tastes terrible!"

Rafferty said, "You see, and all these years you thought I was having a good time!"

Now that you are familiar with various types of verbal wit we can proceed with learning the necessary skills required in the art of storytelling. These essential principles and techniques may not nurture comic genius but they will guide all who wish to improve and will most assuredly lead to bigger and better laughs.

Since methods prescribed for the professional storyteller are different in many ways than those for the amateur, let us begin with guidelines aimed at the non-professional.

FOR THE AMATEUR

You enjoy telling jokes. You love to hear people laugh. It's satisfying to have friends expecting you to tell them the latest gag. Obviously, you are performing some elements correctly. Now let's try to polish and perfect your skill. The first step is to become **aware** of what is required to avoid making unnecessary and embarrassing mistakes.

MEMORIZE THE EXACT PUNCHLINE

Nothing is more frustrating or disappointing than when someone tells a joke and says, "Oh, I forgot the punchline."

The punchline is the most important part of the story. It's the line that ties the entire story together. It makes the point. It's the payoff. It is the catalyst for evoking a response—laughter.

You can change or twist the rest of the story. You can adapt it to fit different occasions or circumstances but you must not change the punchline. Once you have learned it and can say it comfortably the punchline must remain the same.

If you've memorized the exact punchline, no matter how poorly you relate the initial part of the joke you will have the security of knowing you can deliver the punchline correctly. When you read or hear a joke that you like well enough to repeat, learn the punchline first.

One of my closest friends in show business loves hearing as well as telling the latest jokes. When I finish telling him a story he'll laugh at it, enjoy it but while he's laughing he will repeat the punchline. He'll finish laughing, then deliver the punchline again. Then he'll say, "That's funny!" and repeat the punchline once more. It took some time for me to figure out why he was repeating the punchline of the story. He was adding a new story to his collection.

After you've said the punchline out loud three times repeat it thrice more. (In fact, repeating is one of the best ways to remember the entire joke.) Do it while taking a shower or in the bathtub. As you drive to work deliver it three times again. And then, once more for good measure.

You have by now repeated the punchline to your story ten times. It is stamped indelibly in your memory. At this point you can proceed to learn the **set-up**: the beginning and middle which are essential for the punchline to work.

RULE: Memorize your punchline. Get it down letter perfect. Don't spoil your chance to earn a laugh by hesitating, stumbling, recalling, or apologizing.

TELL A STORY IN THE
FEWEST WORDS POSSIBLE

When telling stories *more* words are not better. *Less* is more.

The size of the laugh you get is inversely proportionate to the number of words used to reach the punchline. In other words, the fewer the words the bigger the laughs.

Great storytellers spin yarns without using one extra word. They become great because they learn early on the inviolate rule: Most stories depend on exact wording to be funny.

The ability to edit one's words carefully is the mark of a true professional.

In my interview with Jack Benny for *The Great Comedians Talk About Comedy*, Jack discussed the importance of editing. This was the actual exchange:

WILDE: Could you pinpoint the specific steps you've taken to remain a star all these years?

BENNY: I've always had good shows ... I was the comedian, of course, but I think I was almost a better editor. Most comedians give me credit for being not the best comedian in show business but the best editor ... which is as important as being a comedian. There is nothing as important as editing.

Sometimes unskilled storytellers may not be aware that they are taking too long to get to the point or punchline.

What is the best way to avoid excess verbiage? After choosing your story, get it down pat, make sure every word is in place so that you can tell it without hesitation or self-correction.

RULE: **Make it short and sweet.**
No story got funnier by getting longer.

REHEARSE THE STORY UNTIL
IT BECOMES SECOND NATURE

You can't get an accurate reading of audience response unless you present the material smoothly. You can insure a smooth delivery only through practice.

With practice you can avoid the embarrassment of "not remembering the punchline" or the howls of disappointment when you've left out the salient points of the story.

Here are some specifics:

Repeat the story aloud. Repeat it over and over until you can tell it without the slightest mistake.

If you are really serious about perfecting your expertise, deliver the story into a tape recorder. Listen to it objectively.

Have you told it in the least number of words possible? Practice!

Edit out the unnecessary, flowery sentences. Keep only the main points. Practice!

Tell the joke to your mother-in-law. Tell it to an uncle. The butcher. The mailman. Dial the telephone operator and tell it to her. Anybody who will listen.

There is even a joke to illustrate the point:

A visitor to New York walked up to a newspaper stand and said to the dealer, "How do I get to Carnegie Hall?"
"Practice, mister, practice!" he replied.

RULE: **Practice insures success.**

DON'T LAUGH AT YOUR STORIES

It's the same as applauding for yourself.

It indicates that you are insecure about the funniness of the material and you are trying to help it along.

However, if you've diligently rehearsed the story, if you are satisfied that you're telling it in the least number of words possible and your audience doesn't laugh or the story doesn't quite get the reaction you'd hoped for—get rid of it.

It's time to try something else. That's the fun of story telling: the search for material that will serve you best when you need it.

You must keep trying until you find the right joke that gets the kind of laugh you want it to. Then let the audience enjoy your selection.

RULE: **Do not laugh at your stories.**

DON'T BLAME THE AUDIENCE IF THEY DON'T RESPOND; THE FAULT LIES WITH THE STORYTELLER

Did you memorize the exact punchline?

Did you tell the story in the least number of words possible?

Did you practice telling the story until it became second nature?

Are you still unsure of what happened?

Maybe you told the wrong joke at the wrong time.

It's critical to get the right kind of laugh. You don't want a **shock** laugh which usually follows an off-color story. An **embarrassed** giggle almost always comes from telling a tasteless joke. You must learn to judge your listeners.

Using dirty words for shock value is ill-advised in most social circumstances. A good storyteller who knows his or her audience and is sensitive to their feelings will never revert to vulgarity.

Finding the right jokes and telling them at the right time and place is an acquired awareness. It is an expertise that can be learned only by trial and error.

RULE: **Keep experimenting until you find what works best for you.**

PERSONALIZE YOUR STORIES

Your material will evoke louder and longer laughter if it has a ring of truth to it. If it **sounds** believable. Your listeners want to believe you. The cowboys crowded around the campfire were enthralled with the storyteller. They waited and relied on his every word.

Make your story sound like truth. It doesn't have to be a true story, but it must seem to be true. Very few stories are retold exactly the way they happened. They are embellished and often exaggerated for comedic purposes. But the more truthful the story sounds the more your listeners will get caught up in what you say. One way is to put yourself in it:

> This morning my wife told me about . . .
>
> Let me tell you what happened to me last week as I was coming back from . . .
>
> You won't believe what I saw today at the supermarket . . .
>
> My uncle was the captain of a cruise ship and he told me about this couple who . . .

RULE: **Get listeners more involved by making stories ring true.**

DON'T TELL DIALECT STORIES

Unless you have a really sharp ear to help you reproduce accents, don't tell dialect stories. It is offensive to hear someone tell a story with a bad dialect. To authentically approximate the speech patterns of an older generation Italian, Pole or Irishman requires consummate skill. The listener could easily get the impression that the teller is mocking the particular ethnic group he is trying to imitate.

Instead of being meticulously mimicked, the accent tends to be burlesqued and the result sounds malicious rather than funny.

There are very few dialecticians left in show business. George Jessel, Myron Cohen, Danny Kaye did extraordinary dialects. Of course, they grew up in eastern cities where European immigrants settled and often mangled the English language.

These showmen absorbed the foreign accents of their childhood environment and then, blessed with a good ear, they were able to reproduce them on the stage.

My father was born in Austria. He settled in New York's lower East Side at the age of eighteen. He began learning English from the other immigrants. I grew up hearing him say **oom**possible instead of impossible; **toot**-paste for toothpaste; **adheezum** plaster for adhesive tape. By the time I was a teenager I could imitate perfectly my father's European accent.

The Irishman who lived in our building had a brogue. Mr. Balducci, the proprietor of our nearby fruit and produce store in Jersey City, spoke with a pronounced Italian dialect. While on a two-year tour of Marine Corps duty at Camp Lejeune, North Carolina, and then attending the University of Miami in Coral Gables, Florida, for four years I listened to many "deep South" accents.

During everyday conversation, I practiced delivering different dialects. In order to sound authentic from the speakers platform, I still practice dialects continuously.

Growing up in an environment of many foreign speech patterns gives me some license to duplicate them, but I'm very careful where I use my accents, and I use them sparingly.

It is practically impossible for a native of Kickamule, Texas, to truly capture the inflections and intonations of a Jewish dress manufacturer from New York or a British diplomat from London.

RULE: **Only master storytellers with enormous proficiency can handle dialect stories. Better leave them to the masters.**

FOR THE PROFESSIONAL

The preceding principles were specifically aimed at those who simply enjoy telling jokes at the office, a party or to friends and family in relaxed circumstances. But what about motivational speakers, seminar leaders, sales trainers, people who earn their living from the lecture platform? In addition, there are politicians, executives, members of the clergy and others whose professions require them to speak before audiences.

Although many of the rules are basic approaches to acquiring expertise in the art of story telling they are also invaluable to the professional.

My transition from stand-up comedian to humorous speaker has been a relatively easy one. After more than 30 years of getting laughs in nightclubs, theaters, hotels, fairs, cruise ships, conventions, confirmations and meat market openings, working from the comparatively secure surroundings of the speakers platform is a "piece of cake".

There are many similarities between "performing" and "speaking." Good work habits and the use of time-tested techniques are the indispensable tools for professionals in every field.

Here are some pointers:

MAKE SURE THE AUDIENCE CAN UNDERSTAND EVERY WORD YOU SAY

You can't expect people to laugh if they don't understand what you are saying. To speak clearly and distinctly is an obvious necessity. If you're not careful, sometimes you can slur a key word and the point of the joke is lost.

Another thing that can restrict audience response is improper use of the microphone. This can be deadly when you are depending on audience reaction to bolster your security.

Some time ago I witnessed an attractive young woman showcase at a San Diego National Speakers Association chapter meeting. She used a hand held microphone to speak to more than one hundred members.

The woman was very pleasant, her topic was interesting and she possessed a warm sense of humor. Throughout her talk, she carefully moved her head to the left and then right in order to gain direct eye contact with the audience.

Unfortunately, she committed an egregious error. When she turned her head left or right she neglected to move the microphone with her. Most of the audience couldn't hear her and therefore missed what she was saying. This was particularly evident during the set-up of several funny comments. She moved her mouth away from the microphone and we lost elements that were vital to the punchline. Reaction? Hardly any laughter.

Proper training and continued rehearsal could have turned her talk into something special.

If your object is to get a laugh don't spoil your objective by doing things that will prevent the audience from hearing every word you speak. Clear, concise speech can be learned with practice. So can mike techniques.

In addition be careful not to:

Over gesticulate. (It may draw the audience's attention away from the points you are trying to make.)

Walk around too much while telling the joke. (The movement is disconcerting and may distract the audience's attention.)

These restrictions are offered to improve technical skills. Becoming proficient at them will enhance your understanding of the craft of comedy as well as turn you into a smooth professional. If you are a member of the speaking profession you might find the next rule beneficial.

QUOTE CORRECTLY

When you wish to credit a funny line to its originator quote it **exactly**. All comedy performers strive to perfect their material. Each line is written and rewritten and polished and delivered over and over until it has just the right rhythm and cadence. Each word counts.

When I interviewed Goodman Ace for my book *How The Great Comedy Writers Create Laughter* he said, "You have to put the right word in the right place so the rhythm is there, and the joke makes sense. You can tell a joke to a layman, and he'll repeat it and tell it all wrong. He'll leave out a word or transpose a word."

There is no greater giveaway to a speaker's amateur standing or an indication of his lack of proper preparation than to hear him misquote a famous person.

Mark Twain once declared from the platform:

> "Giving up smoking is the easiest thing in the world. I've done it a thousand times."

Here is the same line delivered by a self-impressed, improperly prepared amateur:

> "Mark Twain once said, 'I've found through my long years of dealing with tobacco that giving up the terrible habit of smoking without question is the easiest thing in the world to do. You're looking at a man who can say without qualification, I've gone and done it myself a hundred times or more."

No self-respecting professional would dare quote the immortal Mark Twain in that manner. Not only is it a breach of integrity, it is, for those who love humor, an unpardonable sin. The joke loses its impact with all those extra words.

If that's not bad enough the joke has lost its impact by adding all those extra words. The laugh is almost totally dissipated.

A speaker using the second example might get away with it but somebody, somewhere will recognize this unspeakable crime. The penalty? Loss of respect. Loss of credibility. Maybe even loss of future bookings.

RULE: **Quote correctly.**

WHERE TO FIND COMEDY MATERIAL

To be a good storyteller you must have a constant supply of material at your finger tips. It's easy to develop a repertoire of satisfactory stories to tell. You have to be on the constant lookout for material. Encourage your friends to tell you jokes. Look for them in the newspapers and magazines. Listen for them on the radio and television.

It's been said that "Adam was a truly lucky man because when he told a joke, he knew nobody had ever heard it before." But there is **no such thing as an old joke**. Always keep in mind that to a person hearing a joke for the first time it is brand new. Most people do not remember jokes. A famous comic known for using the same material for many years used to joke about telling old jokes to his audience: "Folks, I'm not here to tell you new material—I just want to refresh your memory."

Duplicates of modern jokes were told in Biblical times. The speech and formats were different but the ideas were the same. Jokes from *Joe Miller's Jestbook* (1639) are still making the rounds. Although they're wearing a new suit of clothes, the underlying conflicts between husband and wife, parent and child, clergy and congregation, friend and neighbor have never changed. They are the basis for all humor that endures.

There are literally thousands of stories on every conceivable subject. Never be without a good supply. This book contains a collection that will help you keep others laughing for years. You'll find stories on speakers and seniors, politicians and preachers, doctors and lawyers, execs and golfers.

In addition, there is a Humor Bibliography which will provide you with dozens of the most popular joke anthologies in print. A concentrated search will keep you stocked with a pocketful of stories for every occasion.

Developing the skill to be an accomplished storyteller can be inordinately profitable. It can lead to long-lasting popularity with people in the business and professional world as well as in social circles.

Anyone who can amuse and entertain is in great demand for meetings, conferences, conventions, banquets and at a friendly fireside. If you're after fun and profit, it pays to become a master at the art of storytelling.

LARRY WILDE

Speakers' Stories

George Jessel, to whom this book is dedicated, was dubbed "Toastmaster General of the United States" by President Harry Truman. Georgie had a great gift for story telling. He was called upon to speak at political rallies, fund raising dinners and funerals and was in constant demand on the banquet circuit.

George Jessel's eloquence and keen sense of humor have stamped him as the epitome of the professional public speaker. This chapter begins with some classic Jessel joviality.

George, renowned for his eulogies at funerals, was once ribbed by Jack Benny at a Friars' Roast*.

"One of the nicest eulogies I ever heard Jessel deliver was for one of James Mason's cats. You just wouldn't believe what the cat had done for Israel!"

*Show business organization dedicated to raising funds for worthy charities.

Jessel had been asked to speak on behalf of President Roosevelt in a nationwide broadcast. He was allotted twelve minutes, but preceding speakers had exceeded their time limit and the toastmaster general found himself with ninety seconds remaining at the end of the broadcast.

Here's what he said:

"Ladies and gentlemen, most of my eloquent colleagues have this evening taken up much of their time in expounding the weaknesses and vices of President Roosevelt's opponent, Thomas Dewey. I shall not. I could not do this. I know Governor Thomas E. Dewey, and Mr. Dewey is a fine man."

A low murmur of disapproval spread through the assembled crowd.

Jessel went on: "Yes, Dewey is a fine man. So is my Uncle Morris. My Uncle Morris should not be President; neither should Dewey. Good-night."

A young politician approached George and asked, "How do you go about becoming a public speaker?"

Jessel said, "You've got to be able to speak so that people can understand you. You have to practice all the time. One of the best ways is to put a bunch of marbles in your mouth while you talk. Slowly but surely you take away a marble. And then, when you've lost all your marbles, you're a public speaker."

Jessel once opened a Friars' Roast like this:

"As your toastmaster, I'm not going to stand here and tell you a lot of old jokes—but I'll introduce speakers who will."

TOASTMASTER

A man who eats a meal he doesn't want so he can get up and tell a lot of stories he doesn't remember to people who've already heard them.

At a banquet in which Jessel was the main speaker, the M.C. made the mistake of introducing him with a quip, which George felt was slighting: "I am pleased to present a gentleman who has a very glib tongue. All you need to do is put a dinner in his mouth, and out comes a speech."

Jessel rose from his seat and, facing the large audience, he replied:

"Your toastmaster's ability, I must confess, is greater than mine. All you have to do is put a speech in his mouth and up comes your dinner!"

George was toastmaster at a dinner during which the president of the organization was on too long, saying too little. As Jessel began to doze, the lady beside him nudged him.

"Mr. Jessel, would you like some more coffee?"

"Not during his speech," mumbled Jessel. "It might keep me awake."

A Democratic senator running for re-election was giving a speech on a college campus. "Mr. Chairman," he complained, "I have been on my feet nearly ten minutes, but there is so much rowdiness I can hardly hear myself speak."

"It's okay," shouted a student from the rear, "you ain't missin' much!"

Comden asked Baird, who was coming out of the Waldorf Astoria ballroom, "Has the congressman begun speaking yet?"

"Yes," replied Baird, "he's been speaking for half an hour."

"What's he talking about?" asked Comden.

"I don't know," said Baird. "He hasn't said yet."

"Did you hear my last speech?" the presidential candidate asked the reporter.

"I certainly hope so," replied the journalist.

"How did the audience receive your campaign speech when you told them you had never bought a vote?" the campaign chairman asked the Democratic candidate for governor.

"A few cheered, but the majority seemed to lose interest," he replied.

There is only one **ideal** after-dinner speech. It consists of just five words: "I will take the check!"

Campaigning Senator John F. Kennedy had made powerful speeches all over America. One night a man came backstage to meet the handsome Senator. Hoping to gain the secret of Kennedy's tremendous power over his audiences, the man asked, "What is the last thing you do before you go out to deliver one of your lectures? Do you read a favorite passage in Shakespeare or recall an inspiring bit of Shelley's poetry?"

"None of those," replied Mr. Kennedy, "I just feel to see if my pants are zipped up!"

Almost every after-dinner speech has a happy ending— everyone is glad when it's over.

At a Sacramento hotel, a lady recognized the governor pacing up and down and asked him what he was doing there.

"I'm going to deliver a speech."

"Do you usually get so nervous before going on?"

"Nervous?" replied the politician. "No, indeed, I never get nervous!"

"Oh, then," asked the woman, "what are you doing in the Ladies' Room?"

It is always dullest before the yawn.

After a speaker had talked loud and long, he asked the audience if there were any questions. A hand shot up. The speaker nodded.

"What time is it?" asked the man.

Van Gelder, a neighboring vicar, had been called upon to deliver an address at a church dinner. Unfortunately, Van Gelder spoke on and on and on, and everybody was bored to death.

Several notes had been passed to Van Gelder, advising him that his time was up, but he paid no heed.

Finally, the church treasurer grabbed a napkin, scribbled a note and gave it to the speaker.

Immediately Van Gelder stopped talking and sat down. The chairman asked the treasurer, "What did you write?"

"Just four words," confided the treasurer, "Your fly is open!"

Some speakers at banquets are like the horns of a steer: a point here and a point there, and a lot of bull in between.

A Yale University professor was the after-dinner speaker at an academic banquet in England.

"As you know," he began, "I come from Yale, and I want to frame my speech around those four letters."

"Y," said he, "stands for Youth: our society is a young one . . ." and he talked about Youth for fifteen minutes.

"Now A," he said, "is for Ambition, the great American virtue . . ." He spoke for twenty minutes on Ambition.

"L stands for Learning," he announced, and did fifteen more minutes on Learning.

"And E for that great institution, Education ..." He wound up with twenty minutes on Education. As he sat down, he asked his neighbor, "How did I do?"

"I enjoyed it," was the reply, "but I'm glad you're not from Massachusetts Institute of Technology."

>   After the dinner is over,
>   After the waiters have gone,
>   After the coffee and mint-drops,
>   After the very last song;
>   Then come the speeches and laughter,
>   And we settle ourselves for a smoke,
>   In the hope that one of the speakers,
>   Will tell us a really good joke.

After a great many bores had spoken, the last speaker rose to the platform clutching a bulky prepared speech.

The guests could hardly conceal their restlessness. However, the audience cheered when he said, "Friends, it's so late I've decided just to mail each of you a copy of this speech." Then he bowed and sat down.

Applause before a speaker begins is an act of faith.
Applause during the speech is an act of hope.
Applause after his speech is an act of charity.

Flagstad was grossly overweight. But the Rotary Club members loved him in spite of it. They elected him president and a member was announcing the results.

"There is a charming fairy tale that when a baby is born its guardian angel bestows a kiss. If the kiss is on the brow, the child will be very brainy, if on the eyes, very beautiful, if on the hands, very artistic—and so on.

"Now I can't say where the angel kissed our new leader, but I do know he'll make a great president."

Parker had been introduced in flattering terms. He stepped to the podium and said, "Such an introduction prompts two prayers for forgiveness: the first for my introducer, because he has told so many lies; the second for myself, because I have enjoyed it so much."

The speaker went on and on until a guest was so fed up he picked up a bottle and aimed it at the speaker's head.

Unfortunately it missed the speaker and hit the man who was sitting beside him. The blow knocked him out. Immediately some people rushed to bring the fellow around. When he came to, the guest exclaimed, "Please, hit me again. I can still hear his voice."

ORATORY
The art of making deep noises from the
chest sound like important messages
from the brain.

Brudecker was sitting next to a very distinguished man at a large charity dinner at which he was about to speak. His neighbor was not on the list of speakers, so Brudecker said to him, "Oh, I really hate having to make a speech."

"Oh I don't mind a bit," said the man, "I just can't bear listening."

Muriel Humphrey once told her husband, Senator Hubert Humphrey, after a particularly windy speech, "Hubert, you don't have to be eternal to be immortal."

The speaker was handed a note just before he was due to speak. It was from his wife and said simply, "KISS,

Laura." The lady sitting next to him remarked, "How sweet of your wife to remind you of her love just before you have to make an important speech."

"That isn't quite the message," he explained. "What this note means is 'Keep It Short, Stupid!' "

Sometimes the difference between a good speaker and a poor speaker is a comfortable nap.

One of the things that bothers lecturers is the habit some people have of looking at their watches.

A speaker was asked if he was disturbed by the practice.

"No," he replied, "I don't mind—until they start shaking them."

At a banquet, several long-winded speakers covered almost every subject possible.

Then another speaker rose and said, "It seems to me everything has already been talked about. But if someone will tell me what to talk about, I will be grateful."

A voice shouted, "Talk about a minute!"

Speaker: Did you notice how my voice filled the town hall?

Wife: Yes, in fact, I noticed several people leave to make room for it.

One day, in early Rome, a Christian was brought into the arena to be sacrificed to the lions. The Emperor sat in his royal box, the crowd cheered wildly as the lion came to the center of the arena. He made a bee-line for the Christian.

But then an amazing thing happened. The Christian grabbed the lion and whispered in his ear. The lion backed away, at first slowly, then turned tail and ran out of the arena.

Another lion was sent in, then a third. And in both cases the same thing happened.

The Emperor summoned the Christian and asked, "What do you tell those lions that makes them run off? If you'll give me the truth you'll have a full pardon."

"Very simple," shrugged the Christian, "I just tell them, 'Of course, you realize that after you've finished eating me you'll have to make a speech.' "

Did you hear about the wife of a speaker who took her husband's temperature with a barometer instead of a thermometer? It read Dry and Windy.

The best ingredient in the recipe of public speaking is the shortening.

PUBLIC SPEAKING
The art of diluting a two-minute idea
with a two-hour vocabulary.

At an evening fraternal club meeting Halsey, the visiting lecturer, droned on and on, endlessly, in the same monotonous voice. Finally, the bored audience, one by one, departed the lecture hall. Only Reed was left, sitting in the first row.

"Sir," said Halsey when he had concluded his very long speech, "I want to thank you for remaining after everyone else walked out."

"Don't thank me," replied Reed, "I'm the next speaker!"

"His last speech had the audience in the aisles."
"Applauding?"
"No, stretching and yawning."

"He's such a great speaker, I'd rather hear him speak than eat."

"Me, too. I sat at the head table with him. I've heard him eat."

The mind cannot absorb any more than the seat can endure.

During a long lecture Langdon suffered many interruptions from a man in the balcony who kept yelling, "Louder! Louder!"

After the fifth interruption, a man in the first row stood up, looked back, and asked, "What's the matter, can't you hear?"

"No, I can't hear," came the answer from the balcony.

"Well, then be thankful and shut up!"

"How was the Kiwanis speaker?"

"Well, his speech was both good and original. The part that was good was not original and the part that was original was not good."

Two seminar leaders met at a National Speakers Association convention. "You're really a terrific speaker," said the first.

"Thanks, I sure wish I could think of something nice to say about your career."

"You could, if you lied as well as I do."

Why do veteran speakers usually gesture vigorously and walk around and around?

A moving target is harder to hit.

Words are the tools by which a speaker plies his trade. A well-known orator once walked up to Noah Webster, the lexicographer, and said, "Mr. Webster, did you know that 'sugar' is the only word in the English language in which the 'su' is pronounced as if it were 'shu'?"

Webster said, "Are you sure?"

Speak when you are angry and you'll make the best speech you'll ever regret.

After a long and boring series of after-dinner speeches, the audience of salesmen was just about ready to charge the platform en masse. The marketing director rose, and said, "I'm sure you wouldn't want to leave before hearing a word from our West Coast rep, Melvin Quinn."

There was no applause when Quinn stood up. He started his speech with: "Gentlemen, I'm reminded of a story." The audience groaned. "It seems," he went on, "there were two skeletons. For days they had been imprisoned in a dark and dank closet. Finally one skeleton said to the other: 'What are we doing here?'

" 'I don't know', said the other skeleton, 'But if we had any guts we'd get the hell out.' "

Quinn sat down to a cheering ovation.

A visiting minister from England on a lecture tour was interviewed by reporters. He treated them to some of the jokes he was going to use in his lecture. Then he said, "Boys, please don't print those jokes, because if they know them in advance, it will hurt my lecture."

The next day one reporter had this in his column, "Interviewed Reverend Latimer, here on a lecture tour, who told us jokes that cannot be printed."

"Did his speech have a happy ending?"
"Sure, everybody was glad it was over."

Will Rogers, toastmastering at a dinner one evening, was peeved by the lengthy talk of a man whom he had just introduced. After the long-winded bore ended his oratory, Rogers said, "You have just listened to the famous Chinese statesman, On Too Long."

Most of us know how to say nothing . . . few of us know when.

Winston Churchill used to say that there were only two things more difficult than making an after-dinner speech—one was climbing a wall which is leaning towards you, and the other was kissing a girl who is leaning away from you.

Churchill was once asked, "Doesn't it thrill you to know that every time you make a speech the hall is packed to overflowing?"

"It's quite flattering," replied Sir Winston. "But whenever I feel that way I always remember that if, instead of making a political speech, I was being hanged, the crowd would be twice as big."

Fred Allen was listening to a long-winded speaker. After an hour the orator said, "Now, to make a long story short . . ."

"It's too late now," rebutted Allen.

Mark Twain once arrived in a small western town early in the afternoon. He had several hours to spend before dinner and his evening lecture. Twain stopped in at the general store and said to the owner, "Good afternoon, friend. Is there any entertainment here tonight that would amuse a stranger?"

The storekeeper said, "I expect there's going to be some feller giving a lecture. I've been selling eggs all day."

A speaker heard some hissing coming from his audience. He challenged, "There are only three things that hiss. A goose, a snake and a fool. Come forth and be identified."

In general, those who have nothing to say contrive to spend the longest time doing it.

An inexperienced speaker arose in confusion at a Toastmasters' meeting and murmured stumblingly: "M-m-my f-f-friends, when I came here tonight, only God and myself knew what I was about to say to you . . . and now only God knows."

Quincy was trying to explain to his lodge group what Einstein's theory of relativity was all about. After he had spoken for two hours, another lodge member jumped up and said, "Quincy, you're even greater than Einstein himself on relativity. They say there are only twelve people in the whole world who understand Einstein's theory—but nobody understands you."

Storyteller Harry Hershfield was the M.C. at a big New York banquet. He began his remarks to the audience: "My job is to talk to you and your job is to listen. If you finish first, please let me know it."

Milton Berle served as toastmaster for many charity dinners. One night at a Beverly Hills banquet, a waiter brought him a plate of soup.
"Not hot enough," said Milton without touching it. The waiter brought another plate full. Again the comic spoke. "Not hot enough yet." Another plate was brought and again the same cry, "Not hot enough."
The waiter said, "Are you sure it isn't hot enough?"

"Absolutely sure," cracked Berle. "It isn't hot enough as long as you can keep your thumb in it."

LECTURE
Something that can make you feel numb
at one end and dumb at the other.

George Burns played one of his classic tricks on close friend Jack Benny. They were both to speak at a banquet. Benny spoke first for 20 minutes and was a big hit.

When Burns came on immediately afterwards, he said, "Mr. Toastmaster, Ladies and Gentlemen, before this dinner, Jack and I made an agreement to trade speeches. He just delivered mine and I'm grateful for the way you received it. I'm sorry but I've lost Jack's speech and I can't remember a thing he had to say."

He sat down to a standing ovation.

SPEAKER'S PRAYER
"Lord, Thou knowest better than I know myself that I am growing older.

"Keep me from getting too talkative and thinking I must say something on every subject and on every occasion.

"Release me from craving to straighten out everybody's affairs.

"Teach me the glorious lesson that occasionally it is possible that I may be mistaken.

"Make me thoughtful, but not moody; helpful, but not bossy. Though knowest, Lord, that what I want most is a few friends at the end."

A well-known speaker lectured to the members of a literary society, and at the end of his address the treasurer approached him with a check. He politely refused it, saying that the money might be used for some charitable purpose.

"Would you mind," asked the treasurer, "if we add it to our special fund?"

"Not at all," said the speaker. "What is the special fund for?"

"To enable us to get better lecturers next year."

Old lecturers never die—they know they'll see better dais.

"You heard my speech, Professor. Do you think it would improve my delivery if I followed the example of Demosthenes and practiced elocution with pebbles in my mouth?"

"I would recommend quick-dry cement."

"How did Frank's speech go over at the club?"

"The entire audience was hissing him except one man, and he was applauding the hissing."

A motivational speaker was addressing inmates at an asylum when his speech was interrupted by one of them shouting, "Do we have to listen to this nonsense?"

The speaker turned to the keeper and asked, "Shall I stop speaking?"

"No, keep going. It won't happen again," replied the keeper. "That man has only one sane moment every seven years."

It's amazing how an after-dinner speaker can eat chicken and ham and be so full of bull.

OVERHEARD AT A SPEAKERS' CONVENTION

He gives the sort of speech that gives failure a bad name.

He holds people open-mouthed with his speeches. They can't stop yawning.

He speaks straight from the shoulder. Too bad his remarks don't start from higher up.

If he said what he thought, he'd be speechless.

He was such a bad speaker the audience hissed the ushers.

He never opens his mouth unless he has nothing to say.

A speaker has three fees: the one he thinks he ought to get; the one he really gets; and the one he tells the Internal Revenue he gets.

INTRODUCING SPEAKERS

Quiet, please. Quiet, please. Let's come to order. It's time for the speaker. You can enjoy yourselves some other time.

You have heard it said before that this speaker needs no introduction. Well, I have heard him and he needs all the introduction he can get.

You have been giving your attention to a turkey stuffed with sage; you are now about to consider a sage stuffed with turkey.

I would like to present the funniest, most talented, most outstanding speaker and the fellow who wrote this introduction for me ...

In Biblical days, it was considered a miracle when a donkey spoke. Listening to our speaker tonight, you can't help but realize how times have changed.

Next we have a young man who's done so much in so little time, it's kind of hard to exaggerate his accomplishments ... but I'll do my best.

Our speaker needs no introduction. What he needs is a conclusion.

The other day I was in Chicago and heard a disc jockey on the radio named Heck (say last name of person you are introducing). Are you related to him?
They will answer, "No!" To which you reply, "That's strange! You sure look like Heck to me!"

SPEAKERS SPEAK

After an introduction like that, I can hardly wait to hear what I am going to say myself.

An introduction like this is like flattery. And flattery is like perfume . . . it is to be sniffed but not swallowed.

Thank you for your wonderful reception, which I so richly deserve and so seldom get.

AFTER APPLAUSE

I feel like a cow on a cold morning. Thank you for that warm hand.
That one left some of you holding the bag!
Well, at least that's better than the utter joke!

I will speak only fifteen minutes at most because of my throat. Your chairman threatens to cut it.

Every time I stand up to speak my mind sits down!

Nervous? If the butterflies in my stomach ever got together, they could carry me right out of here.

After a dinner program like this, a speaker is like parsley . . . not really needed.

Introduced for a full half hour by the Rotary Club president who fancied himself as an orator, a speaker assured his audience, "Now I know how a pancake must feel after too much syrup has been poured over it."

After a long-winded introduction: The kind remarks of your chairman remind me of the man who was at a formal banquet. He put a large forkful of steaming hot baked potato into his mouth, which he instantly spit out on his plate. He looked around at his shocked fellow guests and exclaimed, "Only an idiot would have swallowed that."

This will be a rather short talk tonight and you can thank three people for it: my partner, who took a forty-five minute speech and edited it down to thirty minutes; my wife, who took the thirty-minute speech and edited it down to fifteen minutes; and my secretary, who took the fifteen-minute speech and lost it.

Thank you for the privilege of speaking to you in this magnificent auditorium. You know the meaning of the word 'auditorium,' don't you? It is derived from two Latin words ... audio, to hear, and taurus, the bull.

And now I'm going to say something in the public interest: Goodnight!

And now in response to a great many requests—Good night, folks!

Reverend Lowell was to address a local women's club about sex. His wife was something of a prude, and he didn't think she'd appreciate having him discuss an intimate subject like sex in public. Finally, he accepted the speaking engagement but told his wife he was going to talk about sailing.

The day after the speech, the minister's wife happened to meet the sponsor of the talk at the super market.

"Your husband," gushed the woman, "gave an absolutely splendid speech last night."

"I'm so glad to hear it. After all, he's so inexperienced in that area."

"Oh come now," she blushed, "he seemed to know a great deal about the subject."

"Maybe . . . but he's only tried it twice. The first time he threw up and the second time he lost his hat."

Ministerial Merriment

The preacher, hoping to get acquainted with one of the new members of the congregation, knocked on the front door of her home one evening.

"Is that you, Angel?" came the woman's voice from within.

"No," replied the minister, "but I'm from the same department."

A TWA Boeing 737 flew into a violent thunderstorm and was soon swaying and bumping around the sky. One very nervous woman sitting next to a clergyman turned to him for comfort.

"Can't you do something?" she demanded.

"I'm sorry, ma'am," said the reverend, "I'm in sales, not management."

SIGN IN FRONT OF A CHURCH
In Business Since the Year One.

"Grand Coulee!" screamed the minister as he hit his finger with a hammer.

40

"Grand Coulee? What do you mean Grand Coulee?" asked his next door neighbor.

"Grand Coulee—that's the world's largest dam, isn't it?" asked the minister.

Preacher: There will be weeping, wailing and gnashing of teeth among the wicked who pass on to the next world.

Parishioner: What about those who haven't any teeth?

Preacher: Teeth will be provided.

The Sunday gospel shouter was in great form. "Everything God made is perfect," he preached.

A hunchback rose from the rear of the auditorium. "What about me?"

"Why," said the preacher, "you're the most perfect hunchback I ever saw."

Two deacons were having a social drink at a bar when they saw their preacher go by. One of them became very upset. "I surely hope he didn't see us," he said.

"What difference does it make?" his friend replied. "God knows we're in here."

"I know," said the first deacon, "but God won't tell my wife."

Did you hear about the preacher who complained that he worked himself to death for Heaven's sake?

Teague and Sterling were discussing their churches one day. Teague said, "By the way, we are firing our pastor."

"Why?" asked Sterling.

"For two reasons," replied Teague. "First, he has a poor delivery, and second, he has nothing to deliver."

When it came time to pass the hat the preacher said to his congregation, "And now brothers and sisters, let us all give in accordance with what we reported on Form 1040."

The Fort Wayne *Journal-Gazette* reported this item by its Logansport correspondent:

Triplets born to the Rev. and Mrs. Glenn Hayden last week are the first in Logansport in a decade. The Rev. Mr. Hayden, an evangelist, is also a salesman for duplicating machines.

After the sermon on free salvation, the minister of a southern black church announced that the collection would be taken by Brother Martin. One of the congregation rose in the back of the church, however, and said, "Parson, you all done said that salvation was free—free as the water we drink."

"Yes, brother," agreed the minister. "Salvation is free, but when we pipes it to you, you gotta pay for the piping."

Pastor: What do we learn from the story of Eutyches, the young man who, listening to the preaching of the Apostle Paul, fell asleep and fell out of a window to his death?

Member: Ministers should learn not to preach too long sermons.

CHURCH SIGN
Try our Pray-As-You-Go Plan!

Reverend Hornbeck found only farmer Felton at his first rural Sunday night service. "What do you think we should do about the service," he asked, "in as much as we have such a small congregation."

"Well, I ain't never been to school very much," said the

farmer. "I don't have much education and I don't know
much about the Bible, but one thing I know, when I promise my cows a load of hay, I always keep my promise."

"Well, come in then, and we will have a service," said
the minister.

Hornbeck was long-winded, and it was an exceptionally
long service. Afterward Hornbeck asked Felton, "What did
you think of the service?"

"Well," said the farmer, "I ain't never been to school,
I'm not educated, and I don't know much about the Bible, but one thing I know, when I promise my cows a load
of hay and only one shows up, I never give it the whole
load."

The Baptist and Christian churches were trying to merge.
All the members of both churches agreed, except one old-
timer.

"No," he said, as he shook his head.

"Why, sir?" asked a preacher.

"Well, my mother and father were Baptists, my grandpar-
ents were Baptists, all of my people were Baptists . . . and
nobody is going to make a Christian out of me now!"

What is the difference between a Southern Baptist and a
Northern Baptist?

A Southern Baptist says, "There ain't no hell."

A Northern Baptist says, "The hell there ain't!"

> A divinity student named Tweedle
> Refused to accept his degree!
> He didn't object to the Tweedle
> But he hated the Tweedle, D.D.

A lost and exhausted climber was walking across a
snowy plateau when he suddenly became aware of a strong

smell of fish and chips. Through the mist ahead he saw a monastery with a priest and a monk standing in the doorway.

"You must be the Friar."

"No, he's the frier and I am the chip monk."

It was noon at the mosque. The high priest was intoning, "There is but one God and Mohammed is His Prophet."

A shrill voice broke in, "He is not."

The congregation turned around and among the sea of brown faces could be distinguished one small yellow face.

The genial priest straightened up and said, "There seems to be a little Confucian here."

A movie queen's personal maid knocked on the door of her portable dressing room and announced, "There's a bishop out here who says he married you in 1978."

"That's funny," mused the star. "I'm practically certain I never married a bishop."

Preacher: If there is anyone in this congregation who likes gin, let him get up. What, Jennifer, do you like gin?

Jennifer: Oh, excuse me, preacher, I thought you said sin.

"Are mosquitoes religious?"

"Yes. They first sing over you and then prey on you."

A carpenter died and went to heaven. He began wandering about and very soon was met by Jesus. "Hello," said Jesus, "you look lost. Can I help you?"

"Well," said the man, "I'm a carpenter and I'm looking for my son."

Jesus said: "Father?"
The carpenter said: "Pinnochio?"

A curate went to his first parish, and was met by the vicar, who said: "Ah, Clappham, you've come just at the right moment. The Parish Mothers are having their weekly meeting in the Hall; you must go down and introduce yourself to them."

When Clappham entered the Parish Mothers' meeting the cackle suddenly stopped, and there was an embarrassed silence. The curate commented, "I see you're all knitting or sewing, but can't someone tell a story or ask a riddle to enliven the proceedings?"

"Yes," said old Mrs. Downey in the corner. "What is it a man stands up to do, a woman sits down to do, and a dog holds out his leg to do?"

The curate turned scarlet and stammered, "I . . . I haven't the . . . least idea."

"Why!" said Mrs. Downey, "to shake hands, of course!"

A minister traveling for the first time on a jet seemed a little nervous.

"Would you like a drink?" asked the stewardess.

"No, thanks," he said. "We're too close to the head office."

SOUTHERN SPIRITUAL

She was only the chaplain's daughter,
but you couldn't put anything pastor.

There once was a pious young priest,
Who lived almost wholly on yeast;
    "For," he said, "it is plain
    We must all rise again,
And I want to get started, at least."

After a long, dry sermon the minister announced that he wished to meet with the Board following the close of the service. The first man to arrive was a stranger. "You misunderstood my announcement," said the minister. "This is a meeting of the Board."

"I know," said the man, "but if there is anyone here who is more bored than I am, I'd like to meet him."

CHURCH SIGN
Going To Heaven?
Get Your Flight Instruction Here

Father Flannery had listened to the confessions of nuns for years. A friend asked what it was like to have such an experience week after week?

He replied with a twinkle in his eyes. "It's like being stoned to death with popcorn."

A minister of a church always left the greeting of strangers to the ushers. One Sunday he noticed a plainly dressed woman in one of the free pews. She sat alone and was clearly not a member of the flock. After the benediction the minister intercepted her at the door.

"How do you do?" he asked, "I am very glad to have you with us."

"Thank you," replied the woman.

"I hope we may see you often in our church home," he went on. "We are always glad to see new faces."

"Yes, sir."

"Do you live in this parish?" he asked.

The girl looked blank.

"If you will give me your address, my wife and I will call on you some evening."

"You wouldn't need to go far, sir," said the woman. "I'm your cook."

Did you hear about the new version of the Bible that's published in Marin County, California?

In this one, Jesus goes to the wedding and makes wine from Perrier.

A cannibal complained to a colleague that he had suffered a bad case of indigestion after eating a Franciscan missionary. "How did you cook him?" asked the second cannibal.

"I boiled him."

"That was your mistake. You should never boil Franciscans. They're friars."

"We will proceed to read from the Book of Numbers," said the preacher as he opened the telephone directory.

There was a long-winded minister who preached from Genesis to Revelation in every sermon.

One day, after having covered almost the whole Bible, he said, "Now we have come to Isaiah—what will we do with him?"

One old man said, "He can have my seat, brother, I'm leaving."

A scrupulous priest of Kildare,
Used to pay a rude peasant to swear,
    He would paint the air blue,
    For an hour or two,
While his reverence wrestled in prayer.

NEWS ITEM

Everyone knows that Boston Bingo Halls are run by Catholics. Allegations were recently made that they were calling out the numbers in Latin to keep the Protestants from winning.

Bloggs, a lifelong resident of Minneapolis, was approached by a man asking him to help the Bible Society.

"Not I," exclaimed Bloggs, "I wouldn't give the Bible Society a dime—you talk about St. Paul all through the Bible—and not a word about Minneapolis."

A Dominican, a Franciscan and a Jesuit were meeting in a room. In the middle of their discussion, the lights went out. Undeterred by the darkness, the Dominican stood up and said, "Let us consider the nature of light and of darkness, and their meaning."

The Franciscan began to sing a hymn in honor of our Little Sister Darkness.

The Jesuit went out and replaced the fuse.

Bishop Bidwell was visiting the state insane asylum. He requested an audience with the lunatic who believed himself to be God. Bidwell was ushered into the presence of a tall octogenarian, with a long white beard. The inmate asked if there was anything he could do for the bishop.

"Yes, there is something," said the bishop. "One question has bothered me for many years. When you said you created the world in six days, did you mean six days as we know them, or six ages, or six eons?"

"Bishop," replied the inmate, "I make it a rule never to talk shop."

Did you know that the Los Angeles Zoo now offers a special service for religious animals:

Dial-A-Praying Mantis.

Selby and Rhodes, two elderly clergymen, were lunching in St. Louis.

"Our calling has changed quite a bit in our time," remarked Selby.

"I didn't realize how liberal religion was becoming," said Rhodes, "until I walked past a church and there in front of the steps was a priest wearing street clothes and fixing her makeup."

On the first day a Catholic sister wore the new contemporary dress adopted by her order, she noticed that the boys in the math class she taught were calmly surveying her legs. She turned to them and quipped, "Well, what did you expect? Wheels?"

Preacher: Please take it easy on the bill for repairing my car. Remember, I am a poor preacher.
Mechanic: I know. I heard you Sunday!

CHURCH SIGN
Wanted: Men, Women and Children To Sit
In Slightly Used Pews Sundays!

A minister surprised his congregation by delivering a ten-minute sermon instead of the usual thirty-minute message.

In concluding he explained, "I regret to inform you that my little fox terrier, who appears to be inordinately fond of paper, this morning ate that portion of my sermon which I have not delivered. Let us pray."

After the service a visitor from another church approached the pastor and said, "Preacher, please let me know if that dog of yours has any pups. If it does, I want to buy one for my minister."

Did you hear about the ministers who formed a bowling team and called themselves the Holy Rollers?

Two rabbis were having lunch. "Some of my congregation is switching over to the Quakers!" complained the first.

"Is that a fact?" said the second.

"Yes, some of my best Jews are Friends."

"Good evening, my young friend," said the clergyman, "do you ever attend a place of worship?"

"Yes, sir, every Sunday night," replied the young fellow. "I'm on my way to see her now."

The only ride Reverend Kilby could get out of the little mountain village was in a mule-drawn carriage. "One thing, though," drawled Dester, the driver, "it's a bad road, and I can't rush my mule, Tyler. Been with me so long he's like a brother to me."

Dester pulled up after a few miles and pointed ahead. "Now, that there hill's too steep for Tyler to climb with both of us in here. You'll have to walk."

Reverend Kilby got out and walked. After the minister got back in, the driver said, "Next hill's even worse. To spare Tyler, this time I'll get out and walk."

A few minutes later, the driver said, "I told you this hill is the worst of all. This time we'll both walk. Tyler's gettin' tired already."

Finally, they reached their destination, mostly by foot. Reverend Kilby wearily paid the driver his fee. Then he said, "I had to come here for the sake of my congregation. You had to come here for the sake of money. But for God's sake, why did we bring Tyler?"

Did you hear about the Jewish boy who quit rabbinical school to become a Catholic priest?

Now his mother introduces him as, "My son, the Father."

CHURCH SIGN
Come Early If You Want
A Backseat!

Father Connolly and Rabbi Gottesman were concluding a theological discussion. As they parted Rabbi Gottesman said, "By the way, what are you giving up for Lent?"

"Matzoh-ball soup!" replied the priest.

Moreland, seriously ill, called for Reverend Dempster. "If you pray for me to recover and I do, I'll give you twenty-five thousand dollars toward the new church you're building."

Dempster prayed and Moreland got well. Although the pastor tried to remind him tactfully of his pledge, he met with no success. Finally, he told him outright, "You promised to give twenty-five thousand dollars for the new church . . ."

"Did I?" said Moreland. "Well, that should give you some idea of how sick I really was."

Potter, a Protestant college student, invited his Catholic chum Casey to attend church with him one Sunday.

Casey was most interested in the Protestant order of service and asked many questions.

When the preacher stepped into the pulpit to preach, removed his watch from his pocket and placed it on the pulpit, Casey asked, "What does it mean?"

The Protestant boy whispered, "It doesn't mean a thing."

Reverend Walford was assailed by a teetotaling preacher for his liberal views about drinking. The minister countered by replying, "There are two drinks mentioned in the Bible, wine: *which gladdeneth the heart of man*, and water: *which quencheth the thirst of jackasses*."

The Creator made us with two ends—one on which to sit, the other with which to think. Our success depends upon which end we use the most. Heads we win, tails we lose.

Pray for the best but prepare for the worst. Note that even churches are equipped with lightning rods.

Simpson, a Baptist Deacon, had advertised a cow for sale.

"How much are you asking for it?" inquired Peck, a prospective buyer.

"Six hundred dollars," said Simpson.

"And how much milk does she give?"

"Five gallons a day," the deacon replied.

"How do I know that she will actually give that amount?" asked Peck.

"Oh, you can trust me," reassured Simpson. "I'm a Baptist Deacon."

"I'll buy it," replied Peck. "I'll take the cow home and bring you back the money later. You can trust me, I'm a Presbyterian Elder."

When the Deacon arrived home he asked his wife, "What is a Presbyterian Elder?"

"A Presbyterian Elder," she explained, "is about the same as a Baptist Deacon."

"Oh, dear," he moaned. "I've lost my cow!"

A minister addressed a Deacon, "I'm told you went to the ball game instead of church this morning."

"That's a lie," said the Deacon, "and here's the fish to prove it."

Preacher Putnam had been delivering a dry, long-winded discourse, completely oblivious to the restlessness of his congregation.

The clergyman was brought quickly back to earth as a

small boy sitting in the front pew lamented in a shrill voice: "Mommy, are you sure this is the only way we can get to heaven?"

Minister: Why don't you come to church now, McTavish?

McTavish: For three reasons. First, I dinna like yer theology; second, I dinna like yer singing; and third, it was in your church I first met my wife.

Did you hear about the missionary who gave a tribe of Congo cannibals their first taste of Christianity?

Father Royce ran into Sullivan on the street, "I'm sorry I didn't see you at church yesterday, Patrick," said the priest.

"Well, Father, it was a wet day and it wasn't fit to turn out a dog. But I sent the wife, Reverend."

CHURCH BULLETIN
Children's Day Observed Next Sunday.
Any parents wishing to have children
at this time must see the minister
no later than Friday.

A group of churchgoers were assembled near the church door for the service just about to begin. From across the street a man shouted, "You are just a lot of hypocrites!"

"Come join us!" said the preacher. "There's room for one more."

Grimes and Maxwell, the leaders of two rival Protestant choirs competing on the following day in the finals of a music festival competition, were comparing notes.

"I have to admit," said Grimes, "that you do have a good choir. Beautiful sopranos and contraltos, strong tenors, baritones and basses, but when we reach that lovely passage 'God is love,' we'll knock the damn spots off your wheezing warblers."

RELIGION
Insurance in this world against
fire in the next, for which
honesty is the best policy.

Duncan was speaking to the prep school graduation class.

"Your headmaster has called me 'Doctor,' which is correct, but I must tell you that I am a Doctor of Literature not Medicine. However, as a title, it has proved amazingly useful at times. Once on board a cruise ship, a very pretty young girl, playing deck tennis, slipped and twisted her thigh. Immediately someone called for a doctor. I rushed forward but a Doctor of Divinity had beaten me to it . . ."

Minister: Now, Timothy, why don't you fight against your longing for drink? When you are tempted, think of your wife Maggie at home.

Timothy: When the thirst is upon me, I am absolutely devoid of fear.

One Sunday, a Southern preacher told his congregation that there were over seven hundred different kinds of sin. The next day he was besieged with mail and phone calls from people who wanted the list—to make sure they weren't missing anything.

Did you hear about the Des Moines couple that separated because of religious differences?

He was a pharmacist and she was a Christian Scientist.

Bishop Bundy was a hypochondriac. While playing chess with a pretty girl one evening, he suddenly collapsed in his chair.

"It's what I've always feared," he gasped. "My whole side is paralyzed."

"Are you sure?" asked the girl.

"Of course," moaned the bishop. "I've been pinching my leg, and I feel nothing—nothing at all."

"Your Grace," said the girl, "that wasn't your leg you were pinching."

Little Darren raised his hand in Sunday School and asked the teacher, "Why didn't God give Moses the Ten Commandments on video?"

Cynthia, sitting behind him, shouted, "You dummy! God didn't know whether Moses had VHS or Beta!"

Reverend Bassett rode into a backwoods town and set up a series of camp meetings. The first evening he asked for a volunteer piano player so the congregation could sing. Donavan volunteered and the hymnals were distributed.

"All right," said the preacher. "Let's all sing 'Onward Christian Soldiers.' "

"Sorry," said the piano player, "I don't know 'Onward Christian Soldiers.' "

"That's O.K.," said the preacher. "We'll just sing 'Jesus Loves Me.' Everybody knows it."

"I don't know that one," said Donavan.

The preacher said, "That's all right. We'll sing 'Rock of Ages.' All of us learned that when we were small children."

"Sorry," said the piano player, "but I guess I don't know that one either."

"That piano player is an idiot," shouted someone in the audience.

"Hold it!" exclaimed Reverend Bassett, "I want that man who called the piano player an idiot to stand up."

No one did.

"If he won't stand up, I want the man sitting beside him to stand up."

No one stood.

Suddenly, old man Thetchel stood up and said, "Preacher, I didn't call the piano player an idiot, and I'm not sitting beside the man who called the piano player an idiot . . . what I want to know is, who called that idiot a piano player?"

Political Persiflage

Garret and his small son were visiting the Capitol building.

"Dad, who is that gentleman?" asked the boy, pointing to a man standing on the dais of the House of Representatives.

"That, son," said Garret, "is the Chaplain of the House."

"Does he pray for the members?" asked the boy.

"No," said Garret, "when he goes into the House he looks around and sees the members sitting there. Then he prays for the country."

Johnny: Pa, what is a politician?
Father: Son, a politician is a human machine with a wagging tongue.
Johnny: What is a statesman?
Father: It is an ex-politician who has mastered the art of holding his tongue.

STATESMAN
A man who can solve grave problems that wouldn't have existed if there were no statesmen.

A politician in love with a nightclub singer employed a detective agency to check up on her. He received the following report:

The young lady has an excellent reputation. Her past is without a blemish. She has many friends of good social standing. The only scandal associated with her is that she has often been seen lately with a politician of questionable character.

"Can't use your story," said the newspaper editor to the new City Hall reporter.

"What did I write that's wrong?"

"You say here that the reform party nominates for mayor the owner of our largest brewery and selects for its candidate for district attorney the president of the local League of Women Voters."

"That's right, Chief. They picked Paul Kendall and Rosemary Grant."

"I don't dispute that. It's the headline you suggest. You want us to have a libel suit?"

"What's the matter with an old proverb: POLITICS MAKES STRANGE BEDFELLOWS?"

A Texas candidate for office, speaking of his opponent, said, "That low-down scoundrel deserves to be kicked to death by a jackass—and I'm just the one to do it."

"I have decided," said the senator to his secretary, "to train my memory."

"What system will you use?"

"I don't know," replied the lawmaker. "I'm looking for one that will enable me, when I am interviewed, to remember what to forget."

Doctor: I'm delighted to tell you that you're the father
            of triplets.
Politician: Impossible! I demand a recount.

A Kansas City youngster, with infinite faith in the Lord,
wrote Him this note:

> I would like to give my mother, who takes
> such good care of me and my six sisters, a
> nice birthday present, but I have no money at
> all, so won't You please send me $100 right
> away.

The boy addressed the envelope *For God* and slipped it
in the mailbox.

Somebody at the Post Office, with a sense of humor,
readdressed it to the White House, where it soon reached
the attention of President Reagan. He promptly sent the
youngster a check for five dollars with a cheery note as
well.

Three days later, the boy wrote another note addressed
to God:

> It was wonderful of You to send me the hun-
> dred dollars I asked for. But why did You send it
> through Washington? As usual, those darn Re-
> publican birds up there deducted 95 per cent
> of it!

"Vote for me!" ranted the Republican candidate at a political rally. "I'll give you the shirt off my back!"

"Oh, no," boomed a heckler from the back row. "We
ain't takin' no more shirt off no more politicians!"

"I see here your son's going into politics."

"Yep. We knew he had to be a politician. Even as a kid

he said more things that sounded good and meant nothing than any kid on the block."

POLITICIAN
He approaches every question with an open mouth.

A surgeon, an architect, and a politician were arguing as to whose profession was the oldest.

"Gentlemen," said the surgeon, "Eve was made from Adam's rib, and that surely was a surgical operation."

"Maybe," said the architect, "but prior to that, order was created out of chaos, and that was an architectural job."

"But," interrupted the politician, "somebody had to create the chaos!"

SIXTH-WARD SERENADE
I Get A Kick-Back Out Of You

Did you hear about the politician who refused to listen to his conscience?

He didn't want to take advice from a total stranger.

Horace Greeley, when he was a young reporter, was assigned to interview a Democratic senator who didn't have the personality or intelligence of a screwdriver.

"I've got nothing to say," said the official.

"I know that," snapped Greeley. "Now shall we begin with the interview?"

The Democratic candidate rushed home and joyfully told his wife, "Darling, I've been elected."

"Honestly?"

"Why bring that up?"

SENATOR'S EXPENSE ACCOUNT
She was "honeychile" in New Orleans,
The hottest of the bunch;
But on the old expense account,
She was gas, cigars and lunch.

A Georgia congressman had checked in at an old-fashioned hotel in New York where dinner came with the room.

On the first evening the southerner sat down and the waiter handed him a menu. The congressman tossed it aside, slipped the waiter a ten dollar bill, and said, "Bring me a good dinner."

The meal tuned out well and so the lawmaker did the same thing each night of his stay in New York. As he pressed the last tip in the waiter's palm he said, "I'm going back to Washington tomorrow."

"Have a good trip, sir," said the waiter. "And when you or any of your friends who can't read come to New York, just ask for William."

A large department store advertised a sale on brassieres, in three basic styles: Democrat, Republican and Liberal. A customer approached a saleswoman and asked, "Aren't those rather strange names for brassieres?"

"Not really," replied the woman. "The Democrat supports the fallen and uplifts the masses."

"The Republican makes mountains out of molehills."

"And with the Liberals your cups runneth over."

A politician nominated at a state convention said that he was so surprised by the nomination that his acceptance speech fell out of his pocket.

During a Hartford municipal campaign, a politician dropped in to see the owner of a stationery store. "Can I count on your support?" asked the politician.

"No," said the owner. "I promised my support to the other candidate."

"Ah," laughed the politician, "in politics, promising and performing are two different things."

"In that case," said the storekeeper, "I'll be glad to give you my promise."

POLITICAL TAXIDERMIST
He stuffs ballot boxes

A Republican member of the House of Representatives and his wife were fast asleep in their upstairs bedroom. Suddenly, she began shaking him.

"Wake up!" she shouted. "I think there's a robber in the house!"

"Impossible!" said her half-asleep husband. "In the Senate, maybe, but never in the House."

Two committee chairmen, each a member of the opposite party, were at the same charity dinner. By chance, they entered the men's washroom at the same time. The Republican washed his hands before urinating. The Democrat washed his hands afterwards.

"A good Democrat," declared the local party leader, "learns to wash his hands *after* he relieves himself!"

"A good Republican," said the other man, "learns not to pee on his hands."

The following scene took place in the home of the state Democratic chairman:

"Doris," announced Blake to his wife, "I'm going to find out what our son wants to be when he grows up. Watch."

Blake put a twenty-dollar bill on the table—that stood for the banking business. Next to it he laid a Bible, representing the ministry. And beside the Bible he placed a bottle of whiskey, indicating a life as a bum.

The parents hid behind the drapes. Their ten-year-old son entered the room, picked up the bill, held it to the light, and replaced it. He fingered the pages of the Bible. Then he uncorked the bottle of booze and smelled the contents.

Then the boy quickly stuffed the twenty-dollar bill in his pocket, tucked the Bible under his arm, grabbed the bottle and strolled out of the room.

"Heaven help us!" exclaimed the father, "he's going to be a Republican!"

"Would you contribute ten dollars to help bury a Democrat?"

"Here's thirty dollars; bury three of them!"

The senator of a southern state bragged at a victory party that this day marked the twelfth time the voters had returned him to power.

"I've been elected a dozen times!" he said puffing his chest way out.

"I guess, Senator," said a Republican voter, "the people of this state are just going to keep electing you over and over again until you learn your job!"

"Why did they provide the Capitol with a rotunda?"

"Because politicians love to run around in circles."

POLITICIAN
Someone who can give you his complete
attention without hearing a word you say.

Democratic Councilman:	My son says he would like a job in your department.
Commissioner:	What can he do?
Democratic Councilman:	Nothing.
Commissioner:	That simplifies it. Then we won't have to break him in.

Two Democrat flunkies were off on a binge. "I'm going to leave this job and I want you to come with me," said one of the men after his eighth drink.

"Oh, really?" remarked his pal.

"Yeah. I know a place in Africa where there's a lot of gold just lying around waiting for someone to pick it up."

"I knew there was a catch to it."

"What's the catch?"

"You've got to bend over!"

DEMOCRAT
Someone who believes you don't have to
fool the people all the time.
Just during the election campaigns.

A group of tourists were looking down into the depths of the Grand Canyon.

"Did you know," said the guide, "that it took over five million years for this great canyon to be carved out of rocks?"

"Oh?" said one of the sightseers. "I didn't know this was a government project."

The foreman on a government job ran short of shovels, so he wired Washington, asking for more. The next day he received this reply:

"No more shovels. Tell the men to lean on each other."

Dear Abby couldn't have printed this letter, but somehow it found its way to a Democratic headquarters bulletin board:

"I'm a Vietnam vet. My mother has epilepsy, and my father's laid up with heart trouble, so they can't work. My two sisters are the sole support of the family. They're hookers in Chicago. My only brother is in the pen for murder and rape. I have two cousins who are Republicans. I'm from the South and my problem is this: I am in love with a belly dancer from a town near ours and I want to ask her to be my wife. Should I tell her about my two no-good Republican cousins?"

OVERHEARD IN THE CLOAKROOM
One Congressman to another: "I liked the straightforward way you dodged those issues."

It's nice to have four years between elections. It takes people that long to regain their faith.

"And how do you account for your recent defeat at the polls, Senator?" asked a cub reporter of the eminent Democrat.

"I was a victim."

"A victim—of what?"

"Of accurate counting!"

A farmer had gotten himself elected to the legislature. After he had served in that law-making body for a month, he came home for a weekend.

"Flora," he said to his wife, "I've discovered one thing about the House. It's the first insane asylum I've ever seen or heard of that's run by the inmates."

"Which way to the restroom?" asked the Democratic congressman.

"Just around the corner," replied the attendant.

"Don't hand me any of that Republican propaganda. I'm in a hurry!"

"There are some things in your speech that I didn't quite understand."

"Probably," replied the Congressman. "Those were the topics I referred to in a confident, offhand way to avoid disclosing that I don't understand them either."

What would be a good way to raise revenue and still benefit the people?

Tax every speech made by a politician in this country.

Youngster:	Father, what is a traitor in politics?
Veteran Politician:	A traitor is a man who leaves the Republican party and goes over to the other one.
Youngster:	Then what is a man who leaves the Democratic party and comes over to the Republicans?
Veteran Politician:	A convert, my son!

A large Republican meeting held in a county seat in Ohio was attended by a small boy trying to sell four young puppy dogs. Finally, a man approached the boy and asked, "Are those Republican pups, my son?"

"Yes, sir."

"Well, then," said the man, "I'll take these two."

A week later the Democrats joined the Republicans for a joint meeting in the same place, and the same boy showed up to sell the two remaining dogs. A Democrat walked up to him and asked, "My little lad, what kind of puppies are these you have?"

"They're Democratic pups, sir."

The Republican who purchased the first two happened to overhear this. "Say," he said, "didn't you tell me that those pups that I bought off you last week were Republican pups?"

"Y-e-s, sir," said the young dog seller, "but these puppies ain't—they've got their eyes open."

REPUBLICAN
A politician who stands for what
he thinks the public will fall for.

A candidate for Congress called upon a minister for his support in the upcoming election.

"Before I give you my decision," said the man of the cloth, "let me ask a question. Do you partake of intoxicating beverages?"

"Before I reply," said the candidate, "tell me, is this an inquiry or an invitation?"

POLITICAL MODERATE
A guy who makes enemies right and left.

A Republican candidate, in a house-to-house canvass, was trying to persuade a man to vote for the ticket.

"No," said the voter. "My father was a Democrat and so was my grandfather, and I won't have anything but the Democratic ticket."

"That's no argument," said the candidate. "Suppose your father and your grandfather had been horse thieves—would that make you a horse thief?"

"No," came the answer. "I suppose in that case I'd be a Republican!"

"What organized party do you belong to?"
"I don't belong to any organized party. I'm a Democrat!"

A panhandler stopped a congressman on the street and asked him for a quarter.

"A quarter won't buy anything these days," the man said. "Don't you want a dollar?"

"No," replied the panhandler, "with all the shady politicians around today, I'm afraid to carry too much cash."

Several top-ranking Republicans had a secret meeting at an exclusive Washington club to decide strategy for beating a bill they all detested. As they got down to business, they noticed that the waiter was stationed near the door. And, he refused to leave.

"If you don't scram this minute," shouted one red-faced congressman, "I'm gonna report you to the manager of this club."

"It was the manager who ordered me to stay here," replied the waiter. "He's holding me responsible for the silverware."

Wouldn't it be wonderful if Washington officials could solve our money problems the way we keep solving theirs?

A Democrat and a Republican were discussing their strategy.

"I'm forever promoting," said the Democrat. "For example, whenever I take a cab, I give the driver a large tip and say, 'Vote Democratic.' "

"My approach is very similar," said the Republican. "Whenever I take a taxi, I don't give the driver any tip at all. And when I leave I say, 'Don't forget to vote Democratic.' "

"What makes you think the Democratic senator is conceited?"

"Well, on his last birthday he sent his parents a telegram of congratulations."

Ronald Reagan called Howard Baker into his office one morning.

"Howard, I realize that some day I'm going to pass on," said the president to his aide. "I'd like you to find a nice burial place for me."

Two weeks later, Baker returned and said, "Mr. President, I've found just the spot. It's on a hill overlooking a beautiful stream. And the sun hits it during the day almost as if you were being spotlighted."

"Sounds good," said Ronnie. "How much?"

"$400,000!"

"What? Four hundred thousand dollars!" cried Reagan. "I'm only gonna be there three days!"

A college newspaper recently suggested that the marijuana question could easily be settled by a joint session of Congress.

A newspaper editor had to correct his youthful reporter.

"Never say that every member of the Fourth Ward Political Club takes graft."

"But they all do."

"Yes, I know," said the editor, "but let's avoid trouble. Say that every member of the club, with one exception, takes graft. Then no member of the club will feel personally offended."

The following headline in a daily paper threw City Hall into an uproar:

HALF THE CITY COUNCIL ARE CROOKS

A retraction in full was demanded for the editor under

threat of a libel suit. But the next afternoon the headline read:

HALF THE CITY COUNCIL AREN'T CROOKS

Richard Nixon was out walking along the beach of San Clemente and decided to go for a swim. He got out beyond the waves and suddenly began drowning.

Three teenage boys happened along, dove into the ocean and pulled Nixon ashore. When he had regained his breath, Nixon thanked the boys. "In appreciation," he said, "I'd be willing to use my influence to help you boys in any way I could. Is there anything special you want?"

"I'd like to go to West Point!" said the boy.

"I believe I can arrange that!" said the ex-President.

"I'd like to go to Annapolis!" said another boy.

"I'll see to it immediately," said Nixon.

"I'd like to be buried in Arlington Cemetery," announced the third boy.

"That's a very strange request," said Mr. Nixon. "Why would you want to be buried in Arlington Cemetery?"

"Well," said the youngster, "when I get home and tell my father who I saved from drowning, he's gonna kill me!"

POLITICIAN
A fellow who finds out how the people are going,
then takes a short cut across a field, gets out
in front, and makes them think he is
leading the way.

Three Washington lobbyists were having lunch at the Bistro Francais in Georgetown. The definition of prestige came up.

"Prestige is when you're at a party and get a phone call from the President because he needs your advice."

"No," said the second lobbyist. "Prestige is when you're

invited to go down to the Oval Office and talk to the President personally."

"You're all wrong," said the third. "Prestige is when you're in the Oval Office, talking to the President, and the phone rings. He picks it up, listens for a minute, and then says, 'It's for you!' "

Politics makes strange bedfellows, but they soon get used to the bunk.

A senator was being shown through a factory producing novelty items. He stopped at the work bench of Collins, a young man building what looked like a horse.

"Say," remarked the law maker, "you seem to be building just the front end of these horses. Why is that?"

"We only build the front ends, sir," said Collins, "then we ship them off to Washington for final assembly."

When Republicans say their candidate is a favorite son, that's the greatest unfinished sentence in history.

CONSERVATIVE
A man who is too cowardly to fight
and too fat to run.

Flanagan knelt in the confessional. "Yes, my son?" said the priest as he slid open the partition.

"Bless me, Father, for I have sinned," Flanagan whispered. "Yesterday I killed two Republican election workers . . ."

"I'm not interested in your politics," interrupted the priest. "Just tell me your sins!"

"You're my second choice," the little old lady said to the Republican candidate.

"Thank you," gushed the politician, "and who is your first?"

"Anybody who is running against you," she replied.

A visitor to Washington had parked his car near the Capitol. As he stepped out he said to a man standing nearby, "If you're gonna be here for the next few minutes, will you keep an eye on my car?"

"Hold on there!" declared the bystander. "Do you realize I am a United States Senator and an official in the Republican party?"

"I didn't know that," said the tourist. "But it's all right. I'll trust you!"

Some elections back, the phone rang at Republican headquarters in Washington.

"Excuse me," said the voice, "can you please give me the name of the Democratic candidate for governor in New Hampshire?"

"Why don't you call the Democratic National Committee?" suggested the clerk. "Surely they'll be able to give you the information."

"This *is* the Democratic National Committee!" replied the voice meekly.

Exorbitant oil company profits helped elect a young lawyer to Congress recently. He debated at a rally. The oft-elected Republican Congressman talked about his service to the poor, his service to the elderly and so on. Then the young Democrat spoke:

"When I was a boy, my pa had a registered bull, and he was rented out for 'service' here, or being sent for 'service' there. I was might curious about what this 'service' was, but pa kept saying I was too young.

"One day my folks were away and a neighbor phoned and said he'd like to have our bull for a while. I figured this'd be my chance to find out what 'service' was, so I brought the bull over myself.

"When I asked the neighbor if I could watch, just like my pa, he told me I was too young, so I left.

"But I sneaked back to the high board corral where they'd taken the bull and I found a knothole.

"Folks, it was through that knothole in that high board fence that I saw what the oil companies have been doing to the people of the U.S. for the past forty years."

He won by a landslide.

You can reach any Democratic senator simply by adding S.O.B. after his name. Some say it stands for Senate Office Building.

Grandma came from New Hampshire forty years ago and settled in Alabama. Despite a husband, 12 children and 33 grandchildren who voted the straight Democratic ticket, Grandma remained a staunch Republican until her dying day.

She had truly been a political embarrassment to her kin.

And now the undertaker called to confirm the funeral arrangements for the old lady. One son-in-law, who was head of the county Democratic party, answered the phone.

"I'm sorry to disturb you," said the undertaker, "but there appears to be some confusion as to whether the body is to be buried or cremated."

"Let's not take any chances," said the party leader. "Do both."

A man was alone in a rowboat on the Potomac, shouting, "No! No! No!"

"Nothing to worry about," said a passing policeman to an observer. "He's just a White House 'Yes man' on vacation."

Logan, the owner of two lovebirds, sent for a veterinarian. "I'm worried about my birds," he announced. "They haven't gone potty all week."

The doctor looked inside the cage and asked, "Do you always line this thing with maps of the United States?"

"No," answered Logan. "I put that in last Saturday when I was out of newspapers."

"That explains it!" replied the vet. "Lovebirds are sensitive creatures. They're holding back because they figure this country has taken all the crap it can stand!"

After reading his prepared statement at a Democratic Party press conference, the blustering senator threw the meeting open for questions.

"Is it true," asked one sarcastic reporter, "that you were born in a log cabin?"

"You're thinking of Abraham Lincoln," replied the senator coolly. "*I* was born in a manger."

Old Abe was also known as a great storyteller. Here are some of his classics:

The Republican editors of Illinois met in convention at Bloomington. Mr. Lincoln attended and was invited to address the meeting. He said he was out of his place; he was not an editor, and had no business there; in fact, he was an interloper.

He said, "I feel like I once did when I met a woman riding horseback in the woods. As I stopped to let her pass, she also stopped, and looking at me intently, said, 'I do believe you are the ugliest man I ever saw.'

"Said I, 'Madam, you are probably right, but I can't help it!'"

"No,' said she, 'you can't help it, but you might stay at home!' "

"There are two things even God Almighty doesn't know; how a Illinois Jury will decide, and how a widow will marry."

—A. Lincoln

Congressman Abraham Lincoln once attended a reception in his honor in Washington. Upon arriving, he placed his tall silk hat, open and up, on a chair in the corner of the small reception hall.

A lady, with a rather large physique and a particularly bountiful derriere, headed straight for the chair and sat down upon the hat, crushing it badly. Lincoln rushed over . . . but too late. The damage had been done.

The woman, taking the hat, thrust it into Lincoln's hands and said indignantly, "Here . . . is this yours?"

"Yes, it is ma'am, but I wish you hadn't done that. I could have told you my hat would not fit you before you tried it on."

This was one of Abe's favorite tales:

"A young man had an aged mother and father who owned considerable property. The young man, being an only son and believing that the old people had outlived their usefulness, killed them both. He was accused, tried, and convicted of the murder.

"When the judge came to pass sentence, he called upon him to give any reason he might have why the sentence of death should not be passed. The young man replied that he hoped the court would be lenient to him because he was a poor orphan!"

Show Biz Baubles

The mother of an actor whose play was going to open on Broadway asked him, "Is the play you're in a comedy or a tragedy?"

"If there are a lot of tickets sold it will be a comedy; otherwise it will be a tragedy."

Sally and Grace, who were chorus girls, were talking backstage at the end of the performance.

"What's wrong with the leading lady?" asked Sally. "She acts mad about something."

"She got only nine bouquets over the footlights," replied Grace.

"Nine?" exclaimed Sally. "That's pretty good, isn't it?"

"Yeah," drawled the other chorine, "but she paid for ten."

It was the first part in five years that Birk had managed to get in any play. True, it was only a small speaking part, but it was a start. The hero was to come on the scene and say, "Did you see this man get killed?" Birk's part was to look the hero straight in the eyes and answer, "I did."

For weeks he practiced with those two words, studying

elocution, practicing facial expressions and intonations. Then came the big night. The hero walked in, glanced at the body on the floor, looked at Birk and asked, "Did you see this man get killed?"

Birk looked straight into the eyes of the hero and said, "Did I?"

The only thing some Broadway actors gain by going to Hollywood is three hours.

A well-known ham actor gave up Broadway and became a surgeon. One morning in front of 200 medical students he removed an appendix so skillfully that they applauded his efforts wildly. So he bowed gracefully and cut out the patient's gall bladder for an encore.

A famous actress, recently married, was in her lawyer's office requesting a divorce not three hours after the ceremony.

"What could have gone wrong in such a short time?" asked the lawyer.

"It happened at the church," sobbed the actress. "He signed his name in the register in bigger letters than mine."

Theatrical people are ruled by temperament, pride and sentiment. That's why they are not understood by businessmen.

A leading lady test-driving a new Cadillac told the salesman that the mirror wasn't positioned properly. "I can't see myself in it. All I can see is the car behind."

Christopher was visiting a psychiatrist.
"What do you do for a living?"

"I'm an actor," replied the patient. "I've been an actor for ten years!"

"Really?" asked the shrink. "I attend all the live theater, all the movies, watch a lot of TV. I don't believe I've ever seen you."

"That's understandable," said Christopher, "I haven't worked in eight years."

"You mean you haven't had an acting job in eight years? My god, man, why don't you give up acting?"

"Give it up? I can't do that, doctor, it's my bread and butter!"

Did you hear about the sad case of the actor who fell off a ship passing a lighthouse? He drowned swimming in circles. He was trying to keep in the spotlight.

Andrea's agent informed her she had gotten the part in a movie about the Revolutionary War.

"What I like about this role," the actress told him, "is that it takes place in 1776. According to my numerologist, my lucky number is twenty-two. And when you add the numbers one, seven, seven, and six, you get twenty-two."

"That's not right," corrected the agent. "When you add those numbers you get twenty-one."

"Forget it. I still want the part."

The chorus cutie told her chums, "My new boyfriend's not much to look at, but he comes from fine stock: General Motors, U.S. Steel, IBM . . ."

A relative of Eddie Murphy had never seen the comedian in a concert. Eddie treated him to a ticket, saying, "Here is your chance to see and hear me on stage in person."

The relative came backstage after the performance. Eddie asked for his reaction. To which his kin replied, "Believe me, Eddie, I did my best not to laugh, but you made me."

A New York theatrical manager called up a famous Italian actress and asked her how much she would take to appear in a play.

"Five thousand dollars a week," she replied.

"Accept five thousand with pleasure," the manager cabled back.

"Five thousand for acting," she wired. "Pleasure extra."

Brenna and Carol were talking about another actress on the way to rehearsals. "The director told Vivian that if she let him kiss her," said Brenna, "he'd give her a small part in his next picture."

"What happened?" asked Carol.

"Well," explained Brenna, "she's going to be the star."

When he was about to present a Broadway play, a producer had a clause put in his contract that he was to approve all the advertising. And he was tough to please! He'd fired seven press agents and thrown out forty ads when his latest hireling entered with a gigantic placard.

"Here it is," he said. The producer took a look at the card.

"Here is the play," it read, "which combines the drama of Eugene O'Neil, the wit of Neil Simon, the naked strength of Tennessee Williams, the intellect of Herman Wouk, and the plot mastery of Arthur Miller. Greater than *Hamlet*, more moving than the Bible, this is a play destined to live forever."

"That's it," said the producer. "No exaggeration. Just the simple truth."

Did you hear about the aging ingenue who thinks the best way to keep her youth is never to introduce him to other girls?

A famous doctor was booked to operate on a patient on coast-to-coast television. The patient died. The doctor apologized to the man's wife, "I'm awfully sorry. This was a routine operation for me. But something happened, and your husband died!"

She said, "Well, that's show biz!"

Ezra and Virgil, two billy goats, found a tin can full of film in the desert. Ezra nuzzled it until the lid came off. The film leader loosened around the spool, and the goat ate a few frames.

Virgil ate some, too. Soon they pulled all the film off the reel and consumed the whole of it.

When nothing was left but the can and the spool, Ezra said, "Wasn't that great?"

"Oh, I don't know," replied Virgil, "I thought the book was better."

HOLLYWOOD
The city where they put
beautiful frames in pictures.

An unemployed actor grew despondent and decided to kill himself. He stood in front of the bedroom mirror and put the gun to his temple. He stood that way for five minutes, then put down the gun and said, "You're much too handsome to die."

Waiter: I'd like to remind you that I sang in one of your shows. Are you surprised to find me here, a waiter?

Producer: No. I remember hearing you sing.

A famous singer known for his having been divorced seven times proposed once more to a pretty Hollywood starlet.

"I like you," she said, "but I've heard so much about you . . ."

"Honey," he interrupted, "don't believe those old wives' tales."

For nearly a year, a Hollywood producer had been looking for a really good story. One day an unknown writer was ushered into his office.

"They tell me you have a great play," said the producer. "Go ahead and read it to me."

This was more than the author expected, for he had a severe stutter. But the chance was too good to miss, and so in spite of his speech handicap, he read the whole play, scene by scene.

When he finished, the producer yelled for his secretary. "Sign this man at once," he cried, "he's got a new twist that's sure box office. Every character in the story stutters!"

Ethel Barrymore was in her dressing room in Hollywood when a studio usher tapped on her door.

"A couple of gals are in the reception room, Miss Barrymore, who say they went to school with you. What shall I do?"

"Wheel them in," said Ethel.

The movie director was talking in his sleep. "Darling, I love you," he said. "You are my life, my heart. More than anything else in the world—"

Then he woke up and saw his wife glaring at him. He pretended he was still asleep, rolled over and murmured, "Cut! Now bring on the horses."

A movie director was shouting at an extra on the set. "Don't bawl her out," warned his aide. "She's a relative."

"Yeah," said the brave man, "and who isn't?"

The producer fell in love with the dumbest chorus girl on earth, and the most beautiful.

"Randy," he said, "you could go a long way if you were real nice to somebody who could do you some good. Like *me* for example."

"Ohh—I think I understand," she cooed. "You want me to be nice to you."

So the next morning when she came to work she brought him a large box of candy.

Did you hear about the persistent actress who made it the hard way to Hollywood—she had talent.

The movie actor wouldn't leave his car to go into the studio lunchroom. He explained that he had a bad memory, might forget the car and be left behind. "Your car number is 1492," said the attendant. "Associate it with Columbus."

The actor got out, entered the lunchroom and was just starting on his dessert when the work whistle blew. "Eh-uh, pardon me," he said aloud. "Can someone tell me what year Columbus discovered America?"

"My goodness," said the starlet, "I just hate to think of my twenty eighth birthday."

"Why?" said her friend. "What went wrong?"

The great Fred Allen described the movie capital like this: "You can take all the sincerity in Hollywood, put it in the navel of a flea and still have room left for two caraway seeds and the heart of an agent."

It's hard to keep a Hollywood marriage secret. News of the divorce is bound to leak out.

A talent agent, usually in the best of spirits, sat despondent in a Beverly Hills restaurant.

"What's the sad look for?" asked one of his friends.

"It's that new client of mine," he answered. "Sings like Sinatra, has a build like Robert Redford and acts like Marlon Brando."

"That's great!" said his friend. "You'll make a million bucks on this guy."

"Guy, my foot," cried the agent. "It's a girl."

A starlet, who had been married three years without having a child, complained to her mother, "The big mistake I made was marrying a director instead of a producer!"

TYPICAL HOLLYWOOD MARRIAGE
The bride keeps the bouquet and
tosses the groom away.

The dazzling movie star was applying for her passport.

"Unmarried?" asked the clerk.

"Occasionally," answered she.

Did you hear about the Hollywood starlet who was married so many times she has a wash-and-wear wedding gown?

Bart and Zach, two Bel Air children, were playing in a pool. "How do you like your new daddy?" asked Bart.

"Fine," said Zach.

"I thought you would," said Bart. "I had him last season."

In Tinseltown, when a movie star tells a child a bedtime story, it usually goes like this: "Once upon a time, there was a mama bear, a papa bear and a baby bear by a previous marriage . . ."

A movie star approached his seven-year-old boy and said, "I'm sorry, son, but tomorrow morning I have to use the chauffeur and limousine for business."

"But Daddy," objected the boy, "how will I get to school?"

"You'll get to school like every other kid in America," answered his father. "You'll take a cab."

A Hollywood producer telephoned another producer.

"Hello?" answered his friend.

"Hi! This is Elliot. How're you doing?"

"Oh," said the friend, "really great! I just sold a screenplay for two hundred thousand, I got a fifty-thousand dollar advance on my novel. I also got a TV series coming on next week, and everybody says it's gonna be a big hit. I'm doin' great. How're you?"

"Okay," said the first producer, "I'll call you back when you're alone."

The unemployed actor was working in the men's room of the Beverly Wilshire Hotel. One evening he came rushing across the lobby and found the unemployed actress who was working in the ladies' room.

"You'll never guess what just happened!" he said. "I was down in the men's room and Francis Ford Coppola came in. He said I had an interesting face and told me to come and see him about a movie he's doing. What do you think of that?"

"Gee," sighed the girl, "I wish he'd come into the ladies' room."

Did you hear about the luscious movie star half the men in Hollywood want to marry? The other half already have.

A screenwriter walked into the producer's office and exclaimed, "Boss, we can't make a movie out of this book. It's about lesbians!"

"So who cares," replied the producer. "Rewrite the script and make them Americans!"

The phone rang in the dressing room of a new starlet. She picked it up.

"Hello? Oh, the movie's going great. Well, for a while I was having an affair with the director. Then his wife found out and got all bent out of shape. She tried to commit suicide, but he said he's through with her. Meanwhile, I've moved in with the publicity man." She looked at herself in the mirror, fixed a curl and said, "Oh, by the way, who's calling?"

Many a starlet has made it to the top because her clothes didn't.

How many movie actors does it take to change a light bulb?

One hundred. One to change the bulb and ninety-nine to say, "I could have done that."

After viewing the rushes of a pretty hopeful's screen test, the producer was less than enthusiastic. "Sweetheart, it'll take an act of Congress to get you into the movies."

The buxom blonde sighed, "That's what I thought. Your apartment or mine?"

First, it was see-through blouses, then topless dancers, then X-rated movies. It looks like the only place people are still covering up in is Washington.

Movie actress to hairdresser: "Tint the gray hair brown, color the black hair strawberry, and put a touch of silver on top so it'll look natural."

Hollywood's best acting is done by stars congratulating Academy Award winners.

A mink died and went to heaven, and St. Peter said he would grant its fondest wish.

"In that case," said the mink, "I'd like a full-length coat made out of movie stars."

"I was talking to three producers yesterday. We discussed the oversupply of theaters. I told them those people were killing the cow that laid the golden fleece."

"Cow that laid the golden fleece? Didn't they laugh at you?"

"Nah. They were movie producers, too."

The movie mogul called a meeting of the board. In his hand he held a newly arrived manuscript. "Gentlemen," he said, "it is the first time in my life I've seen a perfect scenario. There's absolutely nothing wrong with it. Make one hundred copies so I can distribute them to all the other writers so that everybody can see a really perfect script."

He paused, lit a cigar, sat back with a pleased smiled. "And hurry," he added, "before I start rewriting it."

The strip tease dancer was on her honeymoon. The groom put on his pajamas and asked, "Aren't you getting ready for bed?"

"No," she replied. "Not until I get a little applause."

A film producer was selecting a chief for his studio staff. The producer insisted that the person be a college graduate.

He liked an applicant and asked if he had a college education. The answer was affirmative.

"Show me your diploma," demanded the producer.

"Sir," said the applicant, "it's not customary for college graduates to carry diplomas around with them."

"Well, then," demanded the producer, "say me a big word."

A Hollywood writer picked up the phone one day and proceeded to have his ear blasted off by a big producer. The writer listened patiently for awhile, but finally managed to interrupt: "Hey, calm down. If you're not careful, you'll get ulcers."

"I don't get ulcers," screamed the producer. "I give them."

Perhaps the most famous Hollywood perpetrator of the malaprop or just plain inappropriate words was Sam Goldwyn. His remarks are legendary. Here are some classics:

"A verbal contract isn't worth the paper it's written on."

"Anyone who goes to a psychiatrist ought to have his head examined."

On being told his latest actress discovery had very beautiful hands: "Yes, very beautiful hands. I'm thinking of having a bust made of them."

To a long time friend: "Now keep what I'm telling you under your belt."

A Goldwyn employee became a proud father, and told him about it. "So what did you name the boy?" Sam asked.

"John," replied the fellow.

"John? Why John?" screamed Goldwyn. "Every Tom, Dick, and Harry is named John!"

Goldwyn didn't get to be king of Hollywood by being indecisive. When asked why he wouldn't change his mind about a particular script, Goldwyn asserted, "I'm willing to admit that I may not always be right—but I'm never wrong."

Goldwyn was playing golf with Chico Marx for $30 a hole. Chico won the first hole. Goldwyn suggested the second hole be played, for double or nothing. Chico won it. Now Goldwyn owed him $60.

"Double or nothing," said Goldwyn on the third hole.

Chico won $120. They continued to bet and Goldwyn continued to lose.

When the debt had reached $960 Chico said, "I didn't come here to win all this money," he said. "I just want to play golf. Just pay me the $30 you owe me and we'll call it square."

"That's very generous of you," said Goldwyn. "Now I'll match you just once more. Sixty or nothing."

Goldwyn was producing a movie that called for a lavish set. He inspected the set when it was done, and approved everything until he came to a sundial sunken in the center of the garden.

"What's this?" he asked.

"A sundial," explained the workman.

"What's it do?"

So the workman explained how the sun, falling on the

blade, made a shadow which moved around the dial as the sun moved across the sky, thus telling time.

"Well," he said, "what won't you boys think of next?"

W.C. Fields was well known for his long bouts with booze. A friend once asked him if he'd ever suffered the D.T.'s in Hollywood.

"I can't say," snapped Fields. "It's impossible to tell where delirium ends and Hollywood begins."

Maurice Chevalier was once asked, "Why is it that when you meet a young lady, the first thing you do is kiss her hand?"

Chevalier replied, "One has to start someplace."

Orson Welles would occasionally attempt a well-advertised but short-lived diet. During such a period one screen writer remarked to another, "I hear Welles has dropped fifty pounds."

The screenwriter inquired, "On whom?"

Bette Davis was so good as Fanny Skeffington in the picture *Mr. Skeffington*, that one reviewer finished his review with this startling sentence: "No one could ask for more than Bette's Fanny."

An actor died, and his will read:

"I wish to be cremated and have ten percent of my ashes thrown in my agent's face."

A movie-studio president who was not exactly noted for his knowledge of the English language received a well-written story titled *The Optimist*. After reading the manuscript, he called a meeting of the company's most creative minds and announced, "Gentlemen, we got a great story here, but I want all of you to think of something simpler for a title. There ain't many people will know that an optimist is an eye doctor."

The manager of a circus human cannon ball told his client: "You can't quit! Where will I ever find another man of your caliber?"

One day, John Barrymore, at the height of his fame, entered a Beverly Hills men's shop, selected a dozen silk shirts with ties to match, and another dozen pairs of silk pajamas.

"Charge it," he said.

"And the name?" asked the clerk politely.

"Barrymore," said the actor, his voice cold as ice.

"And the first name?" persisted the clerk.

"Ethel!" he snapped.

It was Groucho Marx who, in the middle of a Broadway show, suddenly stepped to the footlights and asked, with anxiety in his voice, "Is there a doctor in the house?"

A man stood up in the tenth row. "I'm a doctor," he said.

"Hi, Doc," smiled Groucho. "How do you like the show?"

A couple of beat-up old acrobats had been closing bills at vaudeville houses with the same act for years. One week they finally made the famous Palace Theatre in New York. At the opening Monday matinee, they stood in the wings while John Barrymore gave his magnificent rendition of Hamlet's most famous soliloquy. The audience went into raptures.

One acrobat turned to his partner and muttered, "Well, if that's the kind of junk they want today, we better work out a new act for next season!"

A reporter knocked on the door of the circus midget who was to be interviewed. He was astonished when a man six-feet tall answered the door.

"Is this the residence of Tom Thumb—Barnum and Bailey's most famous attraction?"

"I'm Tom Thumb, the midget," said the man, "but this is my day off."

There are two things that never live up to their advertising: the circus and sin.

Tony and Ray were working on a twelfth-story scaffolding. A circus manager was passing on the street below. Just as he got under the building he saw Tony do a triple somersault off the top of the scaffolding, followed by a backflip, another double somersault, and landing on his feet. The manager shouted, "That's tremendous! Would you like to work in the circus?"

"Yeah, sure."

"How much do you want?"

"A thousand dollars an act."

"A thousand dollars?"

"Yeah, there's five hundred for me and five hundred for Ray, who hit me on the foot with a hammer."

An actor, desperate for work, applied for a job with a traveling circus.

"Okay," said the manager. "We're supposed to have two gorillas in the show, but one just died. You put on this gorilla costume and pretend you're a gorilla. All you have to do is sit in a cage all day long. Nobody'll ever know the difference."

The actor put on the costume and climbed into the cage. Ten minutes later another gorilla was shoved in with him.

"Let me out of here!" he yelled, shaking the bars.

"Shut up," said the other gorilla. "You think you're the only actor out of work?"

The circus proprietor faced his troupe on Friday and said, "As you all know, business is very bad. Last week I could manage to pay you only half wages. This week things have been even worse."

He stopped for a moment and then, wiping his damp forehead, said, "There is only enough cash to pay three of you this week. The lucky three are Hercules, the strong man; Dave Dauntless, the lion tamer; and Strangler Sam, the champion wrestler."

Colby the circus clown boasted that his brother had developed a new act never attempted before. He had himself shot out of a cannot four times as big as any used by previous stunt men.

"How did he stand the shock?" asked another clown.

"That's hard to say," admitted Colby. "We never found him!"

Did you hear the story about the man on the flying trapeze who caught his wife in the act?

And what about the fat lady at the circus who married the India rubber man?

In three weeks he erased her altogether.

Then there was the guy who married the tattooed lady at the circus because of his insomnia. Now when he can't sleep at night he stays up and looks at the pictures.

An author invited a friend to see the premiere of his new Broadway play. After the performance, the author asked, "Well, Sheldon, how do you like my play?"

"Swell," came the reply, "but I have one suggestion to make. In the last act, where you have the heroine stab her husband with a knife, why don't you have her shoot him with a revolver? It'll not only wake up the audience but also let them know the show is over."

Morgan was continually pestering a William Morris agent to sign his daughter to a contract. "Listen," he pleaded, "my daughter sings exactly like Beverly Sills."

One day Morgan brought a cassette tape and said to the agent, "Come on, we'll play it and you'll hear for yourself. My daughter sings exactly like Beverly Sills."

They put the tape on the stereo. After listening for a few minutes the agent asked, "Isn't that the voice of Beverly Sills?"

"Yes, well my daughter sings *exactly* like that."

The performer was explaining his act to Sam Nugold in the agent's office.

"My act is different," he claimed. "I can fly." Then, he took off, circled the room a couple of times, and made a perfect landing.

"Okay," sneered the agent, "so you can imitate birds! What else can you do?"

McCall went to a theatrical agent with his new act.

"What have you got?" asked the agent.

He called "Elmo!" and in walked a small elephant. "Go to it, Elmo," said McCall.

Elmo whipped out a top hat and cane and began to sing and dance like Fred Astaire. He then did a perfect impression of Gene Kelly in "Singing in the Rain". McCall shouted, "Baryshnikov" and Elmo performed a series of incredible leaps and spins.

McCall said, "Sammy Davis, Jr." and Elmo did his complete act, including Davis's impressions. Then McCall said, "Rich Little" and the elephant did Little's complete act.

Finally, Elmo took them to "Show Business Heaven" and did all the greats, ending with Cantor, Caruso and Jolson.

"Well, what do you think?" asked the elephant's owner.

The agent put his arm on the shoulder of the elephant. "Elmer, er Elmo was it? Look, I've been in this business a long time. I've seen young acts come and go, many of them with lots of talent. Let me give you a piece of advice . . . be yourself."

Marital Monkeyshines

"Woody, you must have a good excuse for the black eye."

"No, Van, if I had a good excuse my wife wouldn't have hit me."

Barney and Ellen stood before a judge.

"Your honor," said Barney, "the officer had no right to arrest us and bring us into court for disturbing the peace. We were just standing in the street having a little difference of opinion. That often happens with man and wife."

"Why didn't you have your quarrel at home instead of in the street?"

"What!" said Ellen. "And break up all the furniture?"

Mrs. McClanahan was telling her troubles to the judge in family court. "The only time my husband ever brought a ray of sunshine into my life," she said, "was when he came home at dawn, slammed the door and the venetian blind fell off the window."

Wife: I baked two kinds of biscuits today. Would you
          like to take your pick?

Husband: No, thank you. I'll use my hammer.

Seldon was brought before the court on the charge of refusing to obey a police officer.

"Why did you refuse to move on when ordered to do so by the officer?" asked the judge.

"Well, your Honor," explained Seldon, "my wife told me to meet her at exactly 12 noon at that spot—and I was forced to choose between man's law and wife's law."

"I'm not myself today," Toland said to his wife.

"Yes," she replied, "I noticed the improvement."

Proctor was not the type to compliment his wife, so she was surprised when he called her an angel. "Why did you call me an angel, dear?" asked Mrs. Proctor.

"Because," he replied, "you're always up in the air, you're continually harping on one thing or another, and you never have a damned thing to wear."

"The other night we got in an argument and I had my wife on her hands and knees."

"Really?"

"Yeah, she was yelling, 'Come out from under that bed and fight, you coward!' "

Cameron, taking a national poll, knocked on the door of a modest suburban house. A man opened it.

"Are you the head of this house, sir?"

He replied, "Until my wife comes back from the supermarket I am."

Merv and Joel, both recently married, were having lunch and comparing their wives. "My Coralie is an angel," said Merv. "She couldn't tell a lie to save her life."

"You lucky man," sighed Joel. "Eunice can tell a lie the minute I open my mouth."

"Good news!" said Mrs. Tewksberry. "I've saved enough money for us to go to Europe!"

"Wonderful!" said her husband. "When do we leave?"

"As soon as I've saved enough for us to come back," explained the wife.

At two a.m. Mrs. Culkin was convinced that she heard a prowler down in the living room.

"Tiptoe down the steps in your bare feet," she said. "Don't turn on any lights. Sneak up on him before he knows what happened."

The dutiful husband put on his bathrobe and, just as he reached the bedroom door, his wife added, "And if you don't get mugged, bring me back a glass of milk."

"Do you permit your wife to have her own way?"

"I should say not. She had it without my permission."

Husband: I've changed my mind.
Wife: Thank Heavens! I hope it works better than the other one.

Franklin spotted a drunk sitting on the front lawn of his house crying like a baby. "What's the problem?" he asked.

"I did a terrible thing tonight," sniffed the drunk. "I sold my wife to a guy for a bottle of Scotch."

"That's a shame," said Franklin. "And now that she's gone, you wish you had her back."

"That's right," said the drunk.

"You're sorry you sold her because you really love her," sympathized Franklin.

"No," said the drunk. "I wish I had her back 'cause I'm thirsty again."

The Paytons were dining out when his wife noticed a familiar face at the bar.

"Matthew," she said, pointing, "do you see that man downing martinis at the bar?"

The husband looked over and nodded.

"Well," the woman continued, "he's been drinking like that for ten years, ever since I jilted him."

"Nonsense," said Payton, "even that's not worth so much celebrating."

Sal ran into Carmine, his old army buddy. After bringing each other up to date Sal asked, "How's your wife?"

"I'm afraid," said Carmine, "I lost my wife in a fire."

"I'm sorry, pal. How did it happen?"

"Well, we were eating lamb flambé when the plate overturned on her dress."

"My God," said Sal, "you mean she burned to death?"

"No. The fire fighters arrived in time and she drowned."

Adelaide was attending a seance.

"Do you believe that departed people can communicate with you?" asked the seer.

"I do," she replied. "My husband sends me alimony every week."

HIGH FIDELITY
A drunk who goes home regularly to his wife.

Malborn sat in his attorney's office.

"Do you want the bad news first or the terrible news?" asked the lawyer.

"Hell, give me the bad news first."

"The bad news is that your wife found a picture worth a hundred thousand dollars."

"That's bad news?" asked Malborn. "In that case, I can't wait to hear the terrible news."

"The terrible news is that it's of you and your secretary."

"Was that your wife who let me in?"

"Who else? Would I hire a maid that homely?"

Did you hear about the very sentimental Hollywood star who wanted to get divorced in the same dress in which her mother got divorced?

On their twentieth wedding anniversary, Bert and Hazel took a trip to Germany. While driving through the Black Forest, they came upon an aging sign that said, "Wishing Well."

The couple pulled over beside an old stone well. Bert read the instructions and, leaning over the well, threw in a penny and made a wish. Then Hazel did the same. However, when Hazel leaned over she lost her balance, tumbled in, and drowned.

"Hey," shouted Bert, "it really works!"

Lady Driver: Do you charge batteries here?

Attendant: Sure do.

Lady Driver: Then put a new one in this car and charge it to my husband.

Jane was fuming as she burst into her neighbor's house. "I'm so mad at Arnold," she cried, "I don't know what to do!"

"Why?" said her friend.

"Last night I dreamed some blonde hussy was flirting with him, and he was purring like a kitten."

"Now, Jane, it was only a dream!"

"I know, but if he acts like that in *my* dreams, what in the world do you suppose he does in *his*?"

Alisa and Gretchen met for lunch the week Alisa returned from her honeymoon. "Weren't you taking an awful chance in telling your husband all about your past mistakes on the day you married him?" asked Gretchen.

"I'll say I was," admitted Alisa. "Some of them almost sobered him up."

Visiting Aunt: Your bride worships you, doesn't she?
Recent Groom: I guess so. She places burnt offerings before me three times a day.

Florence and Twila arranged to have cocktails, and as soon as they met, Twila could see that something serious was bothering her friend.

"Out with it, Florence," she commanded. "What's bugging you?"

"I'm ashamed to admit it," sniffed Florence, "but I caught my husband making love."

"Why let that bother you?" laughed Twila. "I got mine the same way."

"You shouldn't worry like that. It doesn't do any good."

"It does for me! Ninety percent of the things I worry about never happen!"

"My wife talks to herself."

"So does mine, but she doesn't know it. She thinks I'm listening."

Enid and Lucille were pedaling their exercise bicycles at a Houston health club.

"My husband's always playing around," complained

Enid. "It's made me so anxious I can't even eat. I've lost twelve pounds."

"Then why don't you leave him?" asked Lucille.

"Oh, I will," replied Enid, "just as soon as I hit 105."

Liz and Debbie were discussing their husbands' faults.

"We've been married 15 years," said Liz, "and every night after dinner he complains about the food."

"Terrible," agreed Debbie, "does it bother you?"

"Why should it bother me if he can't stand his own cooking?"

"Sir, did the mudpack help your wife's appearance?"

"It did for a few days, but then it fell off."

Higby was driving along the road when he saw a car broken down on the roadside so he stopped and offered his help. Mrs. McElroy was standing beside a flat tire.

Higby changed the tire and when he had almost finished, the woman said, "Be very careful letting the back down."

"How come?" he shouted.

"Be quiet," she whispered, "my husband is asleep in the back seat."

"How're you getting along with your new wife?"

"Great. We have a perfect understanding. I don't try to run her life and I don't try to run mine."

"All my husband does is hunt and drink."

"What is he hunting?"

"Something to drink."

McGonagle and his wife were staying in an Oklahoma City hotel when they were disturbed by a loud noise in the middle of the night.

"Where's the light switch?" shouted McGonagle to his spouse.

"Beside your left hand," she replied.

"Don't be so smart," he snarled. "How can I see which is my left hand in the dark?"

On his way out of church, Hilliard stopped at the door to speak to the minister.

"Would it be right," he asked, "for a person to profit from the mistakes of another?"

"Absolutely not!" replied the pastor.

"In that case," said the young man, "I wonder if you'd consider returning the ten dollars I paid you to marry my wife and me last July."

Florence was fleeing a fire in her home. She carried a dog in her arms.

"Lady," a fireman called to her, "is your husband still in the house?"

"Yes," she said.

"Then why don't you get him out of the house instead of the dog?" demanded the fireman. "Do you want him to burn to death?"

"Don't worry, he won't burn," replied the woman. "He's taking a shower."

"Don't take your trouble to bed with you," was the doctor's advice to a very nervous man.

"But doctor," he replied, "my wife won't sleep alone!"

A week after the robbery, Estelle called the police to report several valuable items missing. The investigating officer asked, "Why did you wait a week? When you found all of your bureau drawers pulled out and clothing scattered around, didn't you suspect a burglar had done it?"

"Why, no, officer," she replied, "I just thought my husband had been looking for a clean shirt."

The wedding went off without a hitch and the preacher wound up with, "I now pronounce you man and wife."

The flustered bridegroom, however, was still in a nervous fog. "Is it now kisstomary," he sputtered, "to cuss the bride?"

The preacher smiled and said, "Not until you've been married for a while."

The newlyweds had their first quarrel, and for several hours neither would speak to the other. Finally, the husband decided to give in.

"Please speak to me, dear," he said. "I'll admit I was wrong and you were right."

"It won't do any good," sobbed the bride. "I've changed my mind."

Whitney had such a bad memory, he kept notes about everything. The problem was he often didn't remember what his notes were about.

While going through his papers one day Whitney came across a puzzling name. He tried but just couldn't figure out who the man was. So Whitney wrote to him and asked, "Do you know me? Was there something I was supposed to do for you?"

The reply read, "You already did. I am your wife's first husband."

Edwina: My husband's an efficiency expert.
Astrio: What's that?
Edwina: Well, if women did it they'd call it nagging.

One Sunday morning, Reverend Barlow was emphasizing the frailties of mankind and the inability to lead a sinless life. He said, "If there is anyone here who feels perfect, please stand up."

Garner stood up in the back of the congregation. The preacher said, "Are you telling us that you are perfect?"

"No," said Garner. "I'm standing up for my wife's first husband!"

MATRIMONY
The only union which permits a woman
to work unlimited overtime
without extra pay.

The reception ended and the newlyweds sneaked off to the suite in their honeymoon resort. After a champagne dinner the groom retired to the bedroom, but the bride pulled a chair up to the window and sat gazing out at the stars.

"Honey," called her impatient husband, "aren't you coming to bed?"

"No," she answered. "My mother told me this would be the most beautiful night of my life, and I don't want to miss a minute of it."

The middle-aged man was shuffling along, bent over at the waist, as his wife helped him into the doctor's waiting room. A woman in the office viewed the scene with sympathy.

"Arthritis with complications?" she asked.

"No," explained the wife, "do-it-yourself with concrete blocks."

"My wife kisses me every time I come home."
"Is that affection?"
"Naw—investigation."

Mrs. Watson turned to Mildred, the hostess at dinner and said, "What a wonderful antique locket you're wearing. Does it contain some memento or family picture?"

"It contains a lock of my husband's hair," said Mildred.

"But your husband is still alive."

"Yes," said Mildred, "but his hair is long gone."

Keating was trying hard to peddle his insurance quota. "You ought to take a policy out on your husband," he told the housewife. "Maybe somebody will put arsenic in his soup someday."

"How much?" she asked.

"The policy?"

"No," she smiled. "The arsenic."

Stafford admitted that things were not going well at home between him and his wife.

"Just be more demonstrative," advised his buddy Brent. "When you go home tonight grab her, kiss her and cuddle her close to you and tell her you love her."

The next day the two met again.

"Well, did you take my advice?" asked Brent.

"Yes," said Stafford.

"How did it work?"

"Not too well. She met me at the door, I hugged her and kissed her and said all the things you told me to. But she started crying and she said, 'The water pipes are frozen, the baby has the flu, your mother's come to visit us, and now you come home drunk.' "

"I should never have got married," said Stanley to his buddies at work. "The wife hates me when I'm drunk, and I can't stand the sight of her when I'm sober."

At a Dubuque theatre in the middle of the movie, a woman let out a shriek, "Oh goodness—I forgot to turn off the iron!"

"Pipe down," snapped her husband. "It can't burn too long—I forgot to turn the faucet off in the tub."

"You say your husband owns property in Las Vegas?"

"Yes, the Desert Inn is holding his luggage!"

"A man is responsible for the good name of his family," said the lecturer. "Is there a man among us who would let his wife be slandered and not rise to her defense?"

One meek little fellow in the back of the room stood up.

"What's this?" exclaimed the speaker. "Would you permit your wife to be slandered and not protest!"

"Sorry," said the man. "I thought you said slaughtered."

Bonnibelle was shopping for her wedding gown.

"Have you been married before?" asked the salesgirl.

"No, why do you ask?"

"When a girl has been previously married, it's customary to wear lavender rather than white."

"Let's see what you have in white with lavender trim."

Riley was charged with deserting his wife.

"You have been found guilty," said the judge. "I'm giving your wife $300 a week."

"That's real nice of your Honor," said Riley. "I'll try to give her a few bucks myself!"

One morning Peacock received a letter that warned, "If you don't send fifty thousand dollars to the above address immediately, we will kidnap your wife and you will never see her again."

Peacock sent the following reply:

Dear Sir,

I haven't got fifty thousand dollars but I'm very interested in your offer.

Lionel went to a doctor for advice about his marital problems.

"So what if she does leave you," counseled the M.D. "There's plenty of fish in the sea."

"Mebbe so, Doc, but my bait ain't what it used to be."

Do you know why so many marriages are in trouble?

Because at the wedding, the bride doesn't marry the best man.

Erskine was driving through a small town when he came upon a huge crowd of men. "What's going on?" he inquired.

"Clem Nolen's mule kicked his mother-in-law in the head and killed her," was the reply.

"Oh, then this is a memorial service."

"Hell no, stranger," replied the townsman. "This here's an auction. Every man in town wants to buy that mule."

"My father pays our rent," complained Mrs. Barnes to her husband, "my mother buys our clothes and my aunt pays for our groceries. My brother helps with the children's school fees and my sister arranges our holidays. I'm ashamed that we can't do better."

"You're right," soothed her husband. "You must have at least two uncles who give us nothing."

Irma and Willard were having their usual nightly knock-down, dragout fight. By 11 o'clock Irma was tired and suddenly reversed her tactics. "In spite of all your faults, Willard," she announced, "I've been in love with you since the moment I met you."

"Rubbish," sneered Willard. "If you had really loved me, you'd have married somebody else!"

"What's the latest dope on Wall Street?"
"My brother-in-law."

Mrs. Berkowitz, shopping in the supermarket, went from counter to counter humming and singing to herself.

"You seem to be very happy," remarked the clerk.

"I have every reason to be," replied the woman. "I got a beautiful home, two lovely children, a nice bank account, my husband's life is insured for $100,000 and his health is far from robust."

New Wife: Did I make your toast too dark, dear?
Husband: I can't tell yet. The smoke is too thick.

Laura was telling her husband that she had put her first-aid lessons to good use that afternoon.

"I was crossing Main Street," she explained, "when I heard a terrific crash. There was a man lying in the middle of the street. He had been thrown from his car. He had a compound fracture of the leg, a fractured skull, and was bleeding heavily. Quick as a flash, all of my first-aid training came back to me."

"What did you do?" asked her spouse.

"I sat down on the curb and put my head between my knees to keep from fainting."

Psychiatrists say girls tend to marry men like their fathers. That's why mothers cry at weddings.

Belinda bought a new wig and thought it would be fun to surprise her husband at the office. She walked in and asked him, "Do you think you could find a place in your life for a person like me?"

"Not a chance," he snapped. "You remind me too much of my wife."

Emily entered a Pittsburgh women's shop and announced that she wanted three outfits for European travel. The saleswoman fitted her out with three complete wardrobes that included hats, gloves, shoes, and purses.

Emily squealed with delight. After spending the entire morning, she thanked the saleswoman politely and said, "Well, those are just the sort of clothes I'll buy if my husband ever lets me go to Europe."

WIFE
A woman who helps her husband out of
scrapes he wouldn't have gotten into in the
first place, if he hadn't married her.

St. Peter stood at the Pearly Gates to welcome a new group of men who had just arrived. He said, "Now, I want all the men who were henpecked on earth to move over to this side."

All the men moved over except Wilford. St. Peter said to him, "Are you the only man who wasn't henpecked on earth?"

"No," replied Wilford.

St. Peter said, "Then why are you standing here?"

"My wife told me to."

Why is it that widows can get married so easily?
Dead men tell no tales.

Moriarty walked into a Boston bar, ordered a martini, and put the olive in a jar. Then he ordered another martini and did the same thing. After an hour, Moriarty was full of martinis, the jar was full of olives and he stumbled out into the street.

"Wow," said a customer, "I never saw anything as weird as that."

"What's so weird about it?" asked the bartender. "His wife sent him out for a jar of olives."

As he went to open the freezer one morning before going to work, Wicksted turned to his wife and asked, "What shall I take out for dinner?"

The woman smiled sweetly and said, "Me."

"How are we going to celebrate our anniversary, honey?"

"How about five minutes of silence?"

Lou met his old friend Ben on the street. "Ben, I haven't seen you in three years. You look terrible. What's happened to you?"

"You won't believe it," said Ben. "I got married three times in the last three years and buried three wives!"

"How tragic," said Lou. "What happened?"

"Well, three years ago I married this rich widow and she died a month later after eating poisonous mushrooms. A year later, I met this wealthy divorcee and she died a month after we were married from eating poisonous mushrooms. Then last year, I married again and believe it or not, after one month she died."

"Don't tell me, poisonous mushrooms?"

"No, fractured skull. She wouldn't eat the poisonous mushrooms."

Small Fry Funnies

"Do you have any children?"

"No."

"What do you do for aggravation?"

You can tell a child is growing up when he stops asking where he came from and starts refusing to tell where he is going.

Walt and Peter were discussing disciplining of their kids.

"Does your son listen to you?" asked Walt.

"Not really," replied Peter. "Ever since he was eight years old, we've been pleading with him to run away from home."

ALLOWANCE
What you pay your children
to live with you.

"What's you son going to be when he graduates?"

"An old man."

Father: What's the matter with Richard?
Mother: He just dug a hole, and now he wants to bring it
          into the house.

Dalton and McGraw were complaining about kids over cocktails.

"Nelda is 16," said Dalton. "I swear she must make 30 phone calls a day."

"You're lucky," said McGraw. "My Susan called her legion of boyfriends so steadily that when she finally got married the telephone company retired her number in her honor."

Children are the light of the house ... but when you have half a dozen, it's time to shut off the light.

Doris, the most talkative teenager in her neighborhood, was burning up the wires one evening on the downstairs telephone, much to the fuming irritation of her father. Finally, after fifteen minutes of the nonsensical conversation between daughter and No. 1 girlfriend, he broke in.

"Doris," he stormed, "I'd like to use the phone. Why in heaven's name don't you use your private phone—the one I got you for Christmas?"

"Gee, Dad," said Doris. "Someone might call me on my phone."

How to keep your teenage daughter out of hot water:
Put some dishes in it.

The teenage girl, after two lessons from the driving school, took her father out for a spin in the family car. "Oh, Daddy!" she trilled. "Doesn't speeding up and down hills make you glad you're still alive?"

"Glad? I'm amazed!"

Walters: What's your son's average income?
Hardy: Between 3 and 4 a.m.

"Doctor," said the pale-faced man to his physician, "I'm in an awful state! Whenever the phone rings, I almost jump out of my skin. The doorbell gives me the shakes. If I see a stranger at the door, I start trembling. I'm even afraid to look at a newspaper. What's come over me, anyway?"

"There, there," said the M.D., "I know what you're going through. My teenage daughter just learned to drive, too."

TEENAGERS
People who regard home as
a drive-in where Dad pays
for the hamburger.

A mother, annoyed because her 15-year-old daughter had been calling her boyfriend too frequently, posted a sign over the telephone: "Is this call necessary?"

Next day there appeared, penciled on the card, "How can I tell till I've made it?"

One teenage girl told another, "I developed an entirely new personality yesterday, but my father made me wash it off."

Did you hear about the teenage girl who has been trying to run away from home for a year, but every time she gets to the front door the phone rings?

Every parent wishes he knew as much as his children think he does, or as much as his children think they do.

Father: What's wrong, Melinda? Usually you talk on
            the phone for hours. This time you only talked
            half an hour. How come?

Melinda: It was a wrong number.

"Do you think your boy will forget all he learned in college?"

"I hope so. He can't make a living necking."

"I want to take my son out of this lousy college."

"But he's at the head of his class."

"That's why I think this is a lousy college."

Grandma Grogan watched her grandson eat his soup with the wrong spoon, grasp the utensils with the wrong fingers, eat the main course with his hands, and pour tea into the saucer and blow on it.

"Hasn't watching your mother and dad at the dinner table taught you anything?" she asked.

"Yeah," said the boy, "never to get married."

They say children brighten up a home. It's true. They never turn off the lights.

"Dad, I raised that twenty dollars I've needed for so long."

"Good work, son. A boy worth his salt should try as early as possible to make himself independent of his father and stand on his own feet. How did you do it?"

"Borrowed it from Mom."

Davenport woke early one morning and decided to surprise the family by making oatmeal for everybody for breakfast.

He was spooning out a bowl for his four-year-old son Freddie. "Want honey on it?" the father asked.

"Yes," said Freddie.

"And milk?"

"Yes."

"Butter, too?"

"Yes."

He gave the bowl to the boy, who just stared at it and pushed it away.

"What's the matter?" asked his dad. "I put everything you wanted on it."

"I don't like oatmeal!" answered Freddie.

Instead of bringing the teacher an apple every day, Bobby, the baker's son, brought her a pretzel. One day she said to him, "These pretzels are very good, but please tell your Dad that they're a little too salty for me."

The next day, she received a pretzel with no salt at all. From then on the pretzels arrived without salt. A month later she said to Bobby, "I hope your father doesn't go to too much trouble, making these pretzels without salt."

"He doesn't make 'em without salt," said the boy. "I lick it off."

"Mom," said the little girl, "can I have a dollar for the poor old man who is standing in front of the house crying?"

"Yes," said her mother. "Here's the dollar. Go give it to him. But, what's he crying about?"

"He's crying, 'Chocolate Dove Bars a dollar a piece.' "

Babysitters say that a good way to keep a child quiet is to let him suck on a bottle of glue.

Candelli, 78, put on his new light tan suit, strolled over to the park, and sat down on a bench to enjoy the spring day.

"What's the matter, sonny?" he asked a small urchin who lay on the grass and stared at him intently. "Why don't you go and play?"

"Don't want to," replied the boy.

"But it isn't natural," said the old man, "for a boy to be so quiet. Why don't you want to?"

"Oh," said the little fellow, "I'm just waitin' till you get up. A man painted that bench about fifteen minutes ago and I want to look at your backside."

Father: My boy, I never kissed a girl until I met your mother. Will you be able to say the same thing to your son?
Junior: Yes, Dad. But not with such a straight face.

Stillwell and Talbot, both fathers of teenagers, were talking about the new generation.

"I attended a wedding ceremony of two high school kids yesterday," said Stillwell, "and the bridegroom wept for an hour."

"How come?"

"It seems the bride got a bigger piece of cake than he did."

Walter: Dick's mother won't let him keep frogs at their house, so he found some water and put them in it.
Mother: Oh, that's fine. Where did he find the water?
Walter: In our bathtub.

Children have become so expensive that only the poor can afford them.

Mrs. Coyle was getting dinner ready when in walked little Kevin with a happy smile on his face.

"What has mama's darling been doing this morning?" asked his mother.

"I've been playing postman," replied the boy.

"Postman!" exclaimed his mother. "How could you do that when you didn't have any letters?"

"Yes, I did," said Kevin. "I was looking through your trunk up in your room and I found a packet of letters tied with a ribbon, and I posted one under every door on the street."

If you wonder where your child left his roller skates, try walking around the house in the dark.

Miles returned to his posh Beverly Hills home from college one hot afternoon and decided to cool off with a dip in the family pool.

"Wait a minute, son," announced his father, "you can't go in the pool with long hair!"

"What?" exclaimed Miles.

"You heard me! It's unhealthy. Get a haircut and you can go in!"

"But, Dad, some of history's greatest men had long hair," said the young man.

"Those are the rules."

"Moses had long hair."

"Moses can't swim in our pool, either."

Zeke was constantly telling lies. One day his father said to him, "George Washington never told a lie. He once chopped down the family cherry tree and when his father asked him if he'd done it he said he did. And his father never punished him because he told the truth."

"Okay, Pa," said the boy, "I'll try to be honest."

One day Zeke felt mischievous. He went down by the river and knocked over the family outhouse. Later, his father found him and said, "Did you push the outhouse in the river?"

"Yep," answered the boy.

His father beat the living daylights out of him.

"Pa," whimpered Zeke, "I thought you said George Washington didn't get no hittin' because he told the truth, about choppin' down the cherry tree."

"Yeah," said the father, "but George Washington's Pa wasn't up the tree when he did it."

Little Harry ran to his mother, sobbing as though his heart would break.

"What's the matter, son?" asked his mother.

"Oh, Daddy was hanging a picture and he dropped it on his toes," the boy said between sobs.

"Why, that's nothing to cry about, you should laugh at that," said his mother."

"I did," replied Harry.

Marcia: Ralphie and I have been downstairs in the dining room, Grandpa. We've been playing husband and wife!

Grandpa: How did you do that, my dear?

Marcia: Well, Ralphie sat at one end of the table, and I sat at the other; and Ralphie said, "This food isn't fit to eat!" and I said, "Damn!" and I got up and left the room!

At a child's birthday party, the hostess had this to say:

"Now remember, kids, there will be a special prize for the little boy who goes home first."

McGee and Wyatt, two college chums, met each other at a school reunion.

"How old are your kids?" asked McGee.

"My children are finally grown up," replied Wyatt. "My daughter started to put on lipstick and my son started to wipe it off."

Mother: Kirk brought you home very late last night.
Ethel: Yes, it was late, Mother. Did the noise disturb you?
Mother: No dear, it wasn't the noise. It was the silence.

Little Oliver tripped and fell on his face on the sidewalk. An elderly lady rushed over to help him to his feet.

"Now, little boy, you must be brave about this," she purred. "You mustn't cry."

"Cry, my foot," replied Oliver, "I'm going to sue the heck out of somebody."

PARENTAL PROVERB
'Tis better to have loved and lost—
than to do homework for three children.

It was the last day of school. A mother walked into her son's room and shouted, "Come on, Huntley, get up! It's time to go to school!"

Huntley pulled the sheets over his head and said, "No! I'm not going! I hate school! I'm sick of school! Sick of it!"

"But, sonny, you have to go!"

"Give me three good reasons why I should go!"

"Well, first of all, you are the principal . . ."

Children are a great comfort in your old age—and they help you reach it faster.

The door-to-door salesman rang the bell in a suburban home and the door opened revealing a nine-year-old boy who was puffing on a long black cigar. Trying to cover his amazement, the salesman said, "Good morning, sonny. Is your mother in?"

The boy removed the cigar from his mouth, flicked off the ashes, and replied, "What do *you* think?"

"I'm worried about my son's health."

"What's he got?"

"A motorcycle."

Every day during summer school the children tried a different kind of meat and their teacher asked them to identify it. On a particular day deer meat was served. No one could guess what it was. Finally the teacher told her class, "O.K., I'll give you a hint. It's what your mother sometimes calls your father."

Gerald jumped up from his seat and shouted, "Don't eat it . . . don't eat it! It's jackass."

Theresa, the mother of seven children, and Colleen, who had five, were discussing their domestic problems as they sipped their mid-morning tea.

"Theresa, I've been meaning to ask you something," began Colleen. "How in the world do you always manage to get your children's attention the way you do?"

"Nothing to it," explained Theresa. "I just sit down and look comfortable."

O'Rourke, the father of 26 children, was voted the father of the year by the Chamber of Commerce.

They gave a celebration in his honor and wined and dined him until long after ten o'clock in the evening. Finally, he got up to make a speech.

"Forgive me if I yawn," remarked the proud papa, "I'm usually in bed this time of night, as you can see by my record."

MIRACLE DRUG
Any medicine you can get the kids
to take without screaming.

An alarmed motorist stopped hurriedly when he saw a teenage boy standing beside a small overturned sports car.

"Anybody hurt in the accident?" he asked.

"There was no accident," replied the youth calmly. "I'm changing a tire."

Hobart, Landrow, and Emory were discussing what most people wanted in a new car.

"Dependability," said Hobart.

"Styling," declared Landrow.

"Economy," said Emory.

Just then a fourth man, who recently had bought a new car, entered the room. They decided to pose the question to him.

"What is the thing you'd like most to get out of your new car?" asked Hobart.

"My teenage son," he replied.

Winthrop and Ames were chatting about their children. "It's getting more expensive every year," said Winthrop. "If I gave the kids everything they asked for at Christmas this year it would cost me a thousand dollars."

"That's one thing about my oldest boy," said Ames. "He just wants only one thing for Christmas this year and it costs only seventy-five cents."

"What in the world will satisfy him that costs only seventy-five cents?" asked Winthrop.

"His own personal set of keys for the car."

"Is your boy a good driver?"

"You might say that. When two cars are double-parked, the one parked by my son is the one on top."

Lady: Oh, isn't he sweet. Little boy, if you give me a kiss, I'll give you a bright new quarter.

Little Boy: I get twice as much at home for just taking castor oil.

The stern-faced middle-aged woman said to a little boy, "Sonny, does your mother know you smoke?"

"Does your husband know you stop and talk to strange men on the street?" replied the youngster.

Children are hereditary. If your parents didn't have any, chances are you won't either.

In a Fort Lauderdale shopping mall, the kindly old lady stopped a toddler and asked, "What's your name?"

"Morris," answered the boy.

"Morris what?" persisted the senior citizen. "What's your last name?"

"My last name?" pondered the little guy. "Oh, I know. Morris Stop That Immediately!"

"From the day your baby is born," counseled a famous scholar, "you must teach him to do without things. Children today love luxury too much. They have execrable manners, flaunt authority, have no respect for their elders. They no longer rise when their parents or teachers enter the room.

What kind of awful creatures will they be when they grow up?"

The scholar who wrote these words, incidentally, was Socrates, shortly before his death in 399 B.C.

Senior Side-splitters

A young reporter interviewed the oldest resident of the state.

"How did you live to be the age of 115?"

"Mainly because I was born in 1873," replied the old man.

Greg and Martha had a busy day receiving well-wishers for their 50th anniversary.

"I'm proud of you," said the husband.

"What did you say?" asked Martha. "You know I can't hear without my hearing aid."

"I'm proud of you!" shouted Greg.

"That's all right," she nodded. "I'm tired of you, too."

At Macy's, an elderly woman picked out two very handsome sweaters—one red and the other blue—and mailed them to her son-in-law Hubert for his birthday. The following week she visited her daughter's house. Hubert was wearing the blue sweater when his mother-in-law arrived.

She looked at him and barked, "What's the matter, didn't you like the red one?"

Did you hear about the wild party they had down at the senior citizen's center?

Things were going rather well until someone decided to perk things up and spike their Geritol punch with prune juice.

OVERHEARD AT A RETIREMENT HOME

She: In most marriage ceremonies they don't use the word "obey" anymore.

He: Too bad, isn't it? It used to lend a little humor to the occasion.

Durward, age 83, who had just been released from jail, ran into his long time crony, Carlisle.

"Where have you been lately?" asked Carlisle. "I haven't seen you around."

"Oh, I've been in jail," replied Durward. "I got arrested, pleaded guilty to rape and they gave me 90 days."

"Isn't that an awfully light sentence for a charge of that kind?" said Carlisle.

"Oh," replied Durward, "they didn't sentence me for rape. They sentenced me for perjury!"

Bob Hope comments on being a senior:

"There are three signs of old age. One is loss of memory. The other two I forgot!"

"Grandpa, why don't you drink tea anymore?"

"A teabag got stuck in my throat once."

Everyone at the Parker family reunion was impressed by the delicious pie that Granny served.

"It not only tastes good," gushed Aunt Millie, "it looks good. How did you make this pretty scalloped crust?"

"It was easy," said Granny. "I used Grandpa's false teeth."

SENIOR CITIZEN SONNET
We're well aware our youth has been spent
That our get-up-and-go has got up and went
But we don't mind, as we think with a grin,
Of all of the places our get-up has been!

Cole and Edith were being driven crazy by Edith's elderly mother who came to spend a weekend and stayed six months.

They decided that Edith would cook a chicken and Cole would pretend it was overdone. They would start an argument and then ask the mother-in-law for an opinion. If she said the chicken was good, Cole would ask her to leave. If she didn't like it, Edith would tell her to go.

That night at dinner the couple began fighting. Suddenly Cole said, "Mom, what do you think of the chicken?"

"I don't know nothin!" exclaimed the old woman, "I'm staying another three months."

Did you hear about the seniors slot machine?
You put in your Social Security check and up come three prunes.

Agatha, aged 75, visited Mosby her physician. "Doctor," she said, "give me a prescription for some of those birth control pills. Then I know I'll be able to sleep."

"But the pill has nothing in it that will affect sleep," said the M.D. "It's for a different purpose entirely."

"Yes. But I know it will help me," she replied.

To humor the old lady Mosby wrote out a prescription for a 30-day supply of the pill. A month passed, and there she was, back again at his office. "Those pills were wonderful!" she exclaimed. "The best rest I've had in years! Give me another month's supply."

"Believe me," said the doctor, "there's absolutely nothing in that pill that can help you sleep."

"Well, my 18-year-old granddaughter lives with me," said the old lady. "Every morning I put a pill in her orange juice and, believe me, I sleep better!"

What's the definition of aging?

When you're not as good as you once were, but you're as good as you were *once*.

Old Halstead complained of severe pains in his left leg. His doctor tried various treatments and medication but the pain persisted.

The old man was becoming impatient. "There must be something you can do for the pain in my leg!"

"Sit down, Mr. Halstead," said the M.D. "Even doctors have their limitations. You understand that, with advancing age, certain deterioration takes place. Try to remember that your leg is eighty-four-years old!"

"Yeah," said the old man, "my right leg is the same age and it doesn't bother me."

At a meeting of seniors, the speaker reached the climax of his talk and declared with fervor: "The time has come when we must get rid of socialism and communism and anarchism, and . . ."

A little old lady stood up, waved her cane and shouted, "And let's throw out rheumatism, too!"

Mabel was a widow, and Wally had recently lost his wife. They hadn't seen each other in 35 years, not since they were graduated from high school, where they had known each other casually. Now, at their high school re-union, Mabel and Wally renewed their acquaintance and, as they chatted, discovered that they had a lot in common. They detested each other.

Penrod, 87, recently married a very young girl. Asked why he risked the result of such disparity in ages, the octogenarian replied, "I'd rather spend the rest of my days smelling perfume than liniment."

Northrop, Garwood and Hadleigh were sitting in Central Park. "I may be 83 years old, gentlemen," said Northrop, "but I'm proud to say that last month my young wife presented me with a baby daughter."

"That's nice," said Garwood. "But I'm 91 and last week my wife gave me a nine-pound boy!"

"Gentlemen," said Hadleigh, "I'm 93! Used to hunt a lot, but I'm too old for that now. However, the other day while walking in the woods I saw a rabbit run by. Well, that old habit took hold of me. I raised my cane and shouted, 'Bang! Bang!' and the rabbit fell over dead.

"Suddenly, another ran by. Again I raised my cane and made the noise of gunfire. Again the rabbit dropped dead. I couldn't believe it. And then, gentlemen, I looked behind me. And there, ten paces to my rear was a young boy shooting with a real rifle."

Dempsey was fifty, Tynan had just turned sixty and they were arguing about Tynan's forthcoming marriage to a girl in her twenties. "I don't believe in these May–December marriages," said Dempsey. "After all, December is going to find in May the freshness and beauty of springtime, but whatever is May going to find in December?"

Tynan replied, "Christmas!"

The sad old tycoon came out of his club, hailed a taxi, and got in slowly and carefully.

The taxi driver asked, "Where to, sir?"

"Drive off a cliff," said the old man. "I've decided to commit suicide."

Sanders was attending a Sacramento Seniors In Retirement dance and he lost his wallet containing $300. "Excuse me," he announced, over the loud speaker, "but I lost my wallet with $300 in it. To the man that finds it I will give $50."

A voice from the rear shouted, "I'll give $75."

Cheryl, a beautiful Michigan State coed, brought home her even more attractive roommate. She introduced the girl to her grandfather. The senior was quite taken by the roommate.

"This is my great grandfather," said Cheryl. "He's in his nineties."

"Early nineties," corrected the old man.

Many a spinster is unmarried because she couldn't stay awake long enough while some man was bragging about himself.

Grandma Phelps was approaching her ninetieth birthday. The children, grandchildren and great grandchildren arrived in Nashville for the gala celebration. "Mother," asked her oldest son, "what would yew like for a present? Just name it? Yew kin have anythin'!"

"Just wanna sit!" replied the old woman.

"How 'bout a ride in an airplane?" suggested another one. "I could arrange the flight."

"I ain't ridin' in no new flyin' machine," said the old

lady. "I'll just sit here and watch television, like God intended I should."

Bertha and Agnes, two Long Island widows, took the bus tour to Mount Vernon, George Washington's beautiful home on the Potomac. They were enthusiastically admiring the various rooms. "And did you notice," said Bertha, "everything is furnished in Early American?"

During the 50th year of their marriage, the Whittakers won a big prize in the state lottery and bought a house in the country. Mrs. Whittaker was showing off their estate to a visiting poor relation from the city.

The visitor looked at the poultry and asked, "Do your hens lay eggs?"

"Yes," said Mrs. Whittaker, "but they don't have to. We can afford to buy them now."

Did you hear about the 92-year-old who married a woman of 84?

They spent the entire honeymoon getting out of the car.

Whitman was visiting his aged father at a Los Angeles retirement home.

"There is one advantage to old age."

"What's that, Pop?" asked Whitman.

"I can sing and brush my teeth at the same time."

An elderly woman in the Bronx recently caused quite a commotion when the contents of her will were revealed. First, she stipulated that she be cremated. Then, she asked that her ashes be spread over Bloomingdale's so she'd be assured of having her daughter visit her at least twice a week.

Did you hear about the man who was so old he chased girls only downhill?

Geriatrics is the science that attempts to solve the age-old problem of old age.

As he completed his physical examination the doctor said to Cromwell, "For a man in his seventies you're in excellent condition."

"Thanks, Doc. Maybe you can help me with my wife. She's got a hearing problem."

"When you go home call to her from the door," advised the M.D. "Then raise your voice and call her again. Then shout it a little louder. Report to me and I'll be able to tell you how severe it is."

Cromwell went home, opened the door and cried, "Dorothy!"

No answer.

Then he yelled, "Dorothy!"

Still no reply.

Cromwell cupped his hands and exclaimed, "Dorothy!!!"

His wife turned to him and said, "Why do you keep shouting? I've answered you three times already."

A visitor to New York City stopped a little old man on 34th Street and said, "Why do they call this the Independent Subway?"

"'Cause it comes when it wants to!" replied the New Yorker.

Peggy and Vern had new neighbors and Peggy was very interested in them. In a few days she reported, "They seem to be a very devoted couple. He kisses her every time he goes out, and even waves kisses to her from the sidewalk. Why don't you do that!"

"Good Heavens!" said Vern. "I don't know her yet."

Milton Berle said on his 79th birthday, "If I knew I was going to live this long, I would have taken better care of myself."

OLD MAID
A girl of advanced age who
goes through life with no hits,
no runs and no errors.

Farber, 78, and Ganz, 81, were passing time on a Pittsburgh park bench.

"How old would a person be who was born in 1940?" asked Farber

Ganz asked, "Man or woman?"

Mrs. Costigan, age 72, visited a doctor and said, "I think I'm pregnant, and want you to verify it."

The physician knew that because of her advanced age, she was imagining things. But he spoke to her kindly, "What makes you think you're pregnant?"

"I know it because I feel life," she said as she patted her stomach.

To humor her, the M.D. asked her to disrobe. After a brief examination, he advised her to go home, take a bath and forget about the pregnancy.

"But doctor," she insisted, "I tell you I feel life and you tell me to go home and take a bath."

"Yes," said the medic, "you've got a bug in your navel."

There was a spinster who said
When she found a thief under her bed,
"I'll let you go free
If you'll marry me."
But he said, "Shoot me instead!"

Old Aunt Melissa staying in a downtown Detroit hotel rang for the manager.

"It's a disgrace," she said to him. "I looked out my window and saw this man and woman fornicating in a room across from mine."

The manager came up, looked out the window and said, "Madam, I can only see the top of that man's head."

"Here," said the old maid, "you just stand on that table."

A genteel spinster named Muir
Had a mind so delightfully pure
  That she fainted away
  At a friend's house one day
When she saw some canary manure.

Miss Millicent passed away at the age of 72. She had never married. The funeral service concluded, and she was carried out by six female pallbearers.

A man said to the funeral director, "I've never seen six woman pallbearers before. Why aren't there any men?"

The director said, "She didn't want any men. She even put it in her will. She said, 'They didn't take me out when I was alive, and they're not going to take me out when I'm dead!' "

Abigail and Adelaide, two elderly sisters, were taking their first trip on a jet. On the 737 Abigail said, "Do you know this plane travels faster than sound?"

Adelaide was quite alarmed about this and when they were settled she said to the flight attendant, "I beg your pardon, Miss, but does this plane travel faster than sound?"

Proudly she said, "Yes, ma'am, we fly faster than sound."

"Well," replied Adelaide, "please slow it down a little, my sister and I want to talk."

SPINSTER
A red hot mama
whose fire has gone out.

"My aunt is an old maid who loves to go to the movies."
"Loves films, huh?"
"No, it's because an usher walks her to her seat—it's the only chance she gets to walk down the aisle with a man."

The world's greatest optimist is the spinster who pulls down a folding bed and then looks under it.

Two elderly women met in the steam room of their Florida condominium.
"Hello, Mrs. Fleigleman, how are you?"
The second woman didn't answer.
"Mrs. Fleigleman, don't you recognize me?"
"You look familiar."
"I'm your next door neighbor."
"Oh, I didn't recognize you without the glasses."

Lucinda had lived a good life, having been married four times. Now she stood before the Pearly Gates.
St. Peter said to her, "I notice that you first married a banker, then an actor, next a minister and lastly an undertaker. What kind of system is that for a respectable Christian woman?"
"A very good system," replied Lucinda. "One for the money, two for the show, three to make ready and four to go!"

Antoinette Carlotta Bologna, the miserly spinster, always opened her morning paper at the Financial Section. Reading that the price of marble was undergoing a temporary slump, she picked up the phone and ordered her tombstone, to be engraved, "DIED A VIRGIN."

"That's eleven letters at $20 a letter," said the cemetery man. "Shall we carve your name above or below the line?"

"Don't carve it at all," snapped the miser. "Why should I waste money, when everybody who reads the message will say, 'That's A. Lotta Bologna!' "

A spinster in silk underwear is like malted milk in a champagne bottle.

Old Aunt Bertha was about to die. She instructed her niece to bury her in her black silk dress, but to cut the back out and make herself a dress.

"Oh, Aunt Bertha," said the niece, "I don't want to do that. When you and Uncle Ethan walk up the golden stairs, I don't want people to see you without any back in your dress."

"They won't be looking at me," replied the old lady. "I buried your Uncle Ethan without his pants."

Two blue-haired old ladies rumbled down the main street of a southern town in their beat-up coupe. They made an illegal turn, and then compounded their crime by ignoring the traffic officer's endeavors to stop them. He finally caught up with them in front of Cora's Ice Cream Shoppe.

"Didn't you hear my whistle?" he demanded.

The perky octogenarian at the wheel said, "Yes, I did officer—but I never flirt when I'm driving."

Old man Kinley was killed in an accident and Simmons was sent to break the news to his wife.

"Be careful how you tell her," advised a friend. "She's a very delicate woman!"

Simmons knocked on the door and she came out. "Pardon me, are you the widow Kinley?"

"Certainly not."

"You wanna bet?"

Bostwick and Meredith, two retirees, were strolling past the home of Armand Hammer. "If only I had that man's millions," sighed Bostwick, "I'd be richer than he is."

"Don't be a dummy," said Meredith. "If you had his millions, you'd be as rich as he is—not any richer."

"You're wrong," said Bostwick. "Don't forget—I could give bridge lessons on the side."

A wealthy widower and his daughter were traveling to Europe on the Queen Elizabeth II. The girl fell overboard. Berman, aged 73, hit the water and saved her. After the two were brought back aboard the ship, the widower threw his arms around Berman.

"You saved my daughter's life," he exclaimed. "I'm a rich man. I'll give you anything. Ask me for whatever you want!"

"Just answer me one question!" said Berman. "Who pushed me?"

Another sign of age is when you feel like the morning after the night before—and you haven't been anywhere.

Dr. Kahn, a New Yorker, was visiting Dr. Beame in his Ft. Lauderdale office when Mrs. Rubin, in her late seventies, entered.

"I have a terrible pain in my stomach," she complained.

Dr. Beame asked her to lie on the table, then he began rubbing her stomach gently. "Around here?" he asked.

"No, more to the side," said Mrs. Rubin.

The M.D. then began soothing the area around her side, although he couldn't find anything the matter with her.

"Perhaps I should have my colleague look you over," said Dr. Beame.

"Certainly," replied Dr. Kahn. He went over to the table and began rubbing Mrs. Rubin's stomach. Soon the old woman got up, put on her sweater and exited the office.

"Aren't you going to prescribe anything for her?" asked Kahn.

"No," he shrugged. "There's nothing the matter with her. She comes in twice a month with the same complaint. She figures at her age how else can she have so much fun for only forty dollars."

Kingsley, age 90, went to a psychiatrist. "How can I help you?" asked the shrink.

"Three months ago I met a beautiful twenty-year-old blonde," explained Kingsley. "I took her home with me and she hugs me and kisses me, she makes love to me 3 times a day—once in the morning, once after lunch and then again at night."

"For a 90-year-old man that's great," said the analyst. "But what's your problem?"

The old man said, "I can't remember where I live!"

"How do you like being a grandfather?"

"I don't mind it at all but I'm not too crazy about sleeping with a grandmother."

The doctor's office was jammed. One elderly patient had to wait a terribly long time. The M.D. apologized to the old man who said, "I didn't mind the wait so much, Doctor, but I thought you'd prefer treating my ailment in its earlier stages."

A women's magazine was taking a survey of married couples: WHAT IS THE SECRET OF A LONG, HAPPY MARRIAGE?

The pollster interviewed a man married 53 years. He said, "Well, my wife and I like to go to dinner twice a week. A good restaurant, candlelight, some soft music, a bottle of wine. Afterward a nice long walk home in the moonlight. She goes Tuesdays and I go Thursdays!"

Frieda and Charles, who were married seventy years, went to a lawyer for a divorce.

"That's incredible," said the attorney, "after being married all these years, why do you want to get a divorce now?"

The old woman said, "We wanted to wait till all the children died."

What do you call a 75-year-old man with herpes?
An incurable romantic.

Wheeler was asked what he was doing now that he is completely retired.

"Not much of anything 'cept working for my wife," said Wheeler. "She pays me three and a half a day."

"Three and a half a day?"

"Yeah! Three meals and half the bed."

Prescott, age 68, explained his predicament to the doctor. He had recently married a gorgeous girl of twenty-six. Unfortunately, every night at bedtime, when he and the bride were ready and willing, he would fall asleep. The doctor scribbled out a prescription and handed it to the patient. Prescott's face lit up and said, "You mean that now I'll be able to . . ."

"No," said the M.D. "I can't do anything about that. But now at least she'll fall asleep, too."

One afternoon in Sun City, Arizona, Melvina turned to her husband of 63 years and said, "I sure could go for some ice cream."

"Just tell me what you want, mother. I'll go get it," said Clovis.

"Why don't you write it down."

"I don't need to write it down. I can remember it."

"I'd like some vanilla ice cream with some hot fudge . . . don't you think you ought to write this down?"

"Don't worry. I won't forget it."

"Okay, I'd like some crushed nuts, some whipped cream and a cherry on top."

He headed out the door and she called, "Darlin', don't you think you ought to write that all down?"

"I told you I don't need to write it down."

He came back 30 minutes later, handed her a paper bag and she pulled out a ham sandwich. She cried, "I knew it! I told you to write it down. You forgot the mustard."

Elderly Lady: Do you have any grandchildren?
Elderly Man: No, all of my children are just ordinary.

A mid-west insurance company discovered that people on New York's lower East Side live longer than they do elsewhere in the nation. So they sent Conway, an actuary expert, down to talk to the residents.

The insurance man found Simonetti, 92, and asked him several questions. Finally, Conway said to him, "Since you've lived here all these years, what would you say the death rate is in this community?"

"Well," said the old man, "I would say it's about one to a person."

"She's thirty-four. I was at her birthday party."
"Were there 34 candles on the cake?"
"There were on the piece I had."

The most priceless antique is an old friend.

SENIOR SENTIMENT
Of all the things I've ever lost,
I miss my mind the most.

The following ad appeared on the third page of the Sunday *Dallas Times Herald*:

"I am fully responsible for all debts and obligations of my wife, Rosalie, both present and future, and am delighted to be the provider for a woman who has borne me three fine children, listened patiently to all my gripes, and with an overabundance of love and care, made the past fifty years of my life the happiest a man could ask for. On this, our fiftieth wedding anniversary, I am proud to express my gratitude publicly."

Medical Mirth

"Is your M.D. a specialist?" asked Boyd.

"He's a family doctor," said Simpson. "He treats mine and I support his."

"I saw the doctor you told me to see."

"Did you tell him I sent you?"

"Yes, I did."

"What did he say?"

"He asked me to pay in advance."

Did you hear about the doctor who was so money-hungry that he put a toll booth on the driveway of his parking lot?

"I gotta admit my doctor knew what he was talking about."

"What do you mean?"

"When I left the hospital he said he'd have me walking in a month. He was right. His bill was so high I had to sell my car."

Sure, people live longer now—
They have to, for goodness' sake,

To pay for doctor bills
And all the pills they take.

"Is your nephew Harold a good doctor?"

"Good? He's such a lovely boy, last year I needed an operation and I couldn't afford it. So he touched up the X rays."

Doctor: You look much better this week.
Patient: I certainly am, Doctor. I reckon it's because I followed the directions on that bottle of medicine you prescribed for me last time.
Doctor: Splendid. What directions?
Patient: It said: "Keep this bottle closed tightly."

Young McCarran strode into the M.D.'s office.

"I just dropped by, Doctor, to thank you," he announced. "I'd like you to know how much I've benefited from your treatment."

The physician asked, "Er—are you one of my patients?"

"No," beamed McCarran, "but my uncle was, and I've just heard his will read."

There is one advantage to being poor—a doctor will cure you faster.

Chatfield was being examined.

"Ah," said the doctor, looking into one eye. "It is easy for me to see what is the matter with you! This is not merely eye trouble; it is an infection of the nervous system. There are all the signs of liver trouble, of fatty degeneration of the heart, of a bad blood supply. The only thing I can recommend is—"

"Say," cried the patient, "isn't it about time you looked into the other eye? That's my glass one."

Every chair in the doctor's waiting room was filled and some patients were standing. At one point the conversation died down and there was silence.

During the silence an old man stood up wearily and remarked, "Well, guess I'll go home and die a natural death."

"I'll never be a success as a doctor," moaned the young surgeon to his mentor.

"Don't be silly," said the Beverly Hills specialist, "of course you will."

"It was a simple appendectomy and I lost the patient. I'll never be a success as a doctor."

"Yes, yes, you will," said the older man. "What did the widow say when you sent your bill?"

"I honestly didn't have the heart to send a bill."

"You're right, you'll never be a success as a doctor."

SPECIALIST
A doctor with a smaller
practice but a bigger yacht.

"What do you think doctors scribble on those prescriptions?"

"That's easy. 'I've got my 60 bucks, now you get yours.' "

"Well, what is the matter with your husband?"

"I think, doctor, he is worrying about money."

"Ah! I think I can relieve him of that!"

Professor:	Now, Mr. Webb, assuming you were called to attend a patient who had swallowed a coin, what would be your method of procedure?
Young Medico:	I'd send for a lawyer, sir. They'll get money out of anyone.

The young athlete visited Dr. Drake. After a cursory examination, the physician assured him that he'd be fine and proceeded to write out a prescription.

"Doctor, I need something to pep me up, something to put me in fighting trim. Will your prescription do that?"

"No, son," answered the M.D., "but my bill will!"

"I saw the doctor today about my loss of memory."

"What did he do?"

"Made me pay him in advance."

"What do you have?" the receptionist asked Dillon in the doctor's waiting room.

"Shingles," he replied.

She gave him a medical form to fill out.

Later, a nurse asked him, "What do you have?"

"Shingles," he repeated.

She sent him into the doctor's office who asked, "What do you have?"

"Shingles," snarled Dillon.

"Where?" asked the M.D.

"Out in the truck. Where do you want me to put them?"

Did you hear about the phony doctor who charges $20 a visit—and more if you're sick?

Wylie sat in Dr. Baxter's examination room. "I don't feel too well," said the patient.

"Strip to the waist and when I hit you on the back, cough."

Baxter hit him and Wylie coughed. For the next 10 minutes every time he hit the patient Wylie coughed. At last the quack said to him, "How long have you had this cough?"

"Yes," the nurse told the anxious caller, "the doctor will consider a house call. What time can you be at his house?"

Dr. Cowdrey was called out to see an elderly man who lived with his married daughter.

"What seems to be the matter with your father?" he asked as he arrived.

"I don't know, doctor," replied the daughter. "He just keeps groaning that he wants to die."

"Aha," said the M.D. "Then you were right in sending for me."

Porter, the son of a general practitioner, had just finished his residency, and his father took him into partnership. A few months later, the old doctor went away on holiday, leaving the young man to look after the practice. On his return Porter informed his father smugly that he had completely cured the back pains which had troubled old Mrs. Spencer for years.

"That's fine, son," smiled his father grimly. "Especially as it was those back pains which put you through medical school."

HERE'S LOOKING AT YOU
An eye specialist in Los Angeles
has just been granted the auto
license number he craved: 2020.

Little Betty climbed on her father's knee and asked, "Daddy, does a doctor ever doctor another doctor?"

"Why do you ask that?" he smiled.

"Because Dr. Warren gave me that nasty-tasting medicine even though I told him I hated it. So I was wondering ... does a doctor doctor a doctor the way a doctored doctor wants to be doctored, or does the doctor doing the doctoring doctor the other doctor the way he wants to?"

"Believe me," said the father, "by the time the doctor first gets his doctorate, he already knows too much about doctors to trust another doctor to doctor him!"

Doctor: Did you ever have it before?
Patient: Yes.
Doctor: Well, you've got it again!

"Does your doctor have lousy handwriting?"
"His prescription is hard to read, but his bill is nice and clear."

The miracle drugs are great. Now a doctor can keep a patient alive until he pays his bill.

OVERHEARD IN A MEDICAL GROUP OFFICE
Senior partner: You seem to have cured the patient. What's worrying you now?
Junior Partner: I filled him up with so many medicines I don't know which one worked.

At Atlanta, thousands of dermatologists gathered for their annual convention. One of the doctors addressed his colleagues by saying, "I guess one could call our business 'itchcraft.'"

McGrath, the chairman of the local fund-raising committee, called on the town's wealthiest doctor, a man well
known for his tightness with a buck. Remarking on the im-
pressive economic resources of his host, the committee
chairman pointed out how miserly it would seem if the
town's richest man failed to give a substantial donation to
the fund-raising drive.

"Let me fill you in on some facts," the medical million-
aire retorted. "I have an eighty-six-year-old mother who's
been hospitalized for the past six years, my widowed
daughter has five young children and no means of support,
and my two brothers owe the government a fortune in back
taxes. Now, I think you'll agree that charity begins at
home."

"I had no idea that you were saddled with so many family debts," apologized McGrath.

"I'm not," replied the doctor, "but you must be crazy to
think I'd give money to strangers when I won't even help
my own relatives."

Dr. Daniels picked up his Cadillac at a garage and was
highly indignant at the size of the repair bill.

"All this for just a few hours' work," he yelped. "You
charge more for your work than we do in the medical profession."

"Well," said the mechanic, "we've got it coming to us.
You guys have been working on the same old model since
time began, but we gotta learn a brand new model every
year."

"I'm afraid," said the heart surgeon, "that you're going
to need a bypass operation."

The patient squirmed uneasily in the seat.

"I'd like a second opinion, if you don't mind."

"Not at all," replied the surgeon. "You're also as ugly as sin."

IN A PHOENIX PHYSICIAN'S WAITING ROOM
An apple a day doesn't do it.

It was just after midnight, and there was a knock on Dr. Lerman's door. Dragging himself out of bed and poking his head from the window he shouted down at the lone figure. "Well?"

The woman looked up. "No, sick."

Dr. Roche was such a busy man that at the hospital he only had time to scribble abbreviations on the patients' charts. T stood for tonsillectomy, OH was open heart surgery, BS meant brain surgery, and so on.

As was his habit, Dr. Roche also greeted new interns as soon as they arrived. Unfortunately he was a little late in getting to Dr. Slade. Greeting the intern in the corridor after surgery, he asked, "So, Dr. Slade, how did Mrs. Crane's appendectomy go?"

Slade paled. "Appendectomy? I thought you wanted an autopsy."

It was 2 a.m. and the phone was ringing.

"Doc!" cried the caller, "my arm got broke in two places! What should I do?"

The sleepy GP replied, "Don't go back to either of them."

One afternoon at the corner drugstore a pretty girl came in and asked the pharmacist to read a letter for her. It was a rather intimate letter, and the girl blushed while she listened. When the pharmacist finished, she gave him a hug and a kiss, then rushed happily out of the store.

"Don't think she's an illiterate," explained the druggist to a waiting customer. "She's a senior at Vassar. But her boy-friend is a doctor, and only a pharmacist like me can make heads or tails of his handwriting."

CONSULTATION
A medical expression that
means share the wealth

Did you hear about the medical prescription written in the usual doctor's fashion?

The patient used it for two years as a pass on the Long Island Railroad. Twice it got him into Radio City Music Hall and once into Shea Stadium. It came in handy as a letter from his employer to the cashier to increase his salary. And his brother-in-law played it on the piano and won a scholarship to the Milan Music Conservatory.

O'Brien walked into his shrink's office and said, "Doctor, my wooden leg hurts!"

The doctor said, "How come?"

O'Brien said, "My wife hits me over the head with it!"

Webster went to see a psychiatrist. "What's troubling you?" asked the doctor.

"Nothing," said Webster, "but my family thought I should come because I like cotton socks."

"Lots of people like cotton socks," said the headshrinker. "As a matter of fact, I like cotton socks myself."

"You do?" cried Webster. "How do you like yours, with oil and vinegar, or just a squeeze of lemon?"

A very homely young woman made an appointment with a psychiatrist. She walked into his office and said, "Doctor, I'm so depressed and lonely. I don't have any friends, no man will touch me, and everybody laughs at me. Can you help me accept my ugliness?"

"I'm sure I can," replied the shrink. "Just go over and lie face down on that couch."

Mitchell, suffering from amnesia, went to see a psychiatrist. "It should be a very simple matter to cure you," said the doctor. "My fee will be $100 an hour."

Mitchell screamed, "You just shocked me into remembering who I am and the guy I am can't afford to pay that kind of money."

Constance had been undergoing psychiatric treatment for some time when she asked the doctor if it was all right for her to go to Hawaii. He gave his approval. A short time later the shrink received the following telegram:

HAVING A WONDERFUL TIME. WHY?

A man lamented, "I always thought talk was cheap until I started talking to a psychiatrist!"

Halston went to a doctor snapping his fingers. The doctor said, "Why are you snapping your fingers?"

Halston replied, "I'm keeping the elephants away!"

The doctor said, "Why that's silly. There isn't an elephant within 500 miles of here!"

"You see! It works!"

Sheen took his wife to the doctor. The M.D. took Mrs. Sheen and hugged her and squeezed her and kissed her then said to her husband, "You see, that's what your wife needs. At least three times a week. Monday, Wednesday, Friday!"

Sheen said, "O.K. Doc, Monday and Wednesday will be all right but Friday she'll have to take the bus!"

FRIENDLY BRITISH PSYCHIATRIST
He lies down on the couch with you;
that's what they call socialized medicine!

Did you hear about the psychiatrist who uses the shock treatment?

He gives his patients the bill in advance.

Doctor: Have you ever had a serious illness?
Patient: No.
Doctor: Ever had an accident?
Patient: No.
Doctor: You mean you have never had a single accident in your life?
Patient: Never, except last spring when a bull tossed me over a fence.
Doctor: Well, don't you call that an accident?
Patient: No, sir! He did it on purpose.

Dr. Weinberg wanted to know what Fanelli could have eaten to necessitate the use of a stomach pump.

"I dunno, Doc," said Fanelli. "I only had a light between-meal snack: six hamburgers, with no relish or nothin', three orders of fries, a couple dozen jelly dough-nuts, and three, four cups-a coffee."

"I thought so," said the physician, "overindulgence!"

"Naw! Over in Jersey!"

"Did you have a good sleep last night?" asked the doctor of an insomniac.

"I slept all right, but it didn't do me any good; I dreamed that I was awake all night."

Chapman, a country doctor, stopped in the small town general store. The owner said, "Mornin' Doc, Where ya been?"

"Oh, I was up North for a week of hunting."

"Kill anything?"

"Not a darned thing," said the M.D.

"Gosh," said the storekeeper, "you could've done better'n that stayin' home and tendin' to your regular trade."

Plotnik sat in Dr. Hiller's office.

"Doctor," he said, "I ain't feelin' too good. I'm here for a checkup."

"Okay," said the physician, "what are your eating habits?"

"Well," said Plotnik, "in the morning I have grape juice, some orange juice, a little prune juice, and then a little cereal—maybe two bowls. After that I have eight, ten rolls. Then I have a half dozen eggs, and a cup of coffee. For lunch, I have some chopped chicken liver, two plates at the most, a bowl of soup, a piece of duck, some cabbage salad, six rolls and a cup of coffee. At supper, I start out with a three-pound lobster, some meat balls, some chicken, a little stew, half a loaf of bread, and pie with a little ice cream, not more than two scoops, and a cup of coffee. What I'd like to know, doctor, am I drinking too much coffee?"

"Farmer Grange, I can't come out to see you anymore."

"Why, what's the matter, doctor?"

"Why, every single time I come out, your ducks insult me."

Nurse: What did you operate on that man for?
Doctor: $3,000.

Dr. Bradshaw's son barely pulled through college. It was only because the father was a former president of the state medical association that he was accepted under pressure by a medical school.

Somehow he managed to scrape through his four years with lackluster grades. On the final day the dean called young Bradshaw in for a serious talk about his future.

"You have," said the dean, "a complete lack of understanding of medicine and a general absence of knowledge about the human body. It is our recommendation you become a specialist."

God heals—the doctor takes the fees.

There had been a flu epidemic in the town. Dr. Morton, who had almost no sleep for a week, called upon a patient who was suffering from pneumonia.

"Begin counting," directed the physician as he leaned over to hear the patient's respiration.

The doctor was so fatigued he fell asleep with his head on the sick man's chest.

It seemed but a moment when he awoke suddenly to hear the patient still counting, "12,840 ... 12,841 ..."

"What are you taking for your cold?"
"I don't know. What will you give me?"

A doctor advised Fogarty to drink warm water an hour before every meal. At his next appointment, Fogarty reported that there had been no improvement in his condition.

"Did you follow my instruction to drink warm water an hour before every meal?" inquired the doctor.

"I'm afraid not," admitted the patient, "I tried, but I can only keep it up for about fifteen minutes."

Surgeon: I'm afraid your condition is critical. I shall have to remove half of your large bowel.

Patient: That's all right, doctor—better a semi-colon than a full stop.

"I had an operation and the Doc left a sponge in me."

"Got any pain?"

"No. But, boy, do I get thirsty!"

PATIENT'S PROGNOSIS
I'll take ten trains to a doctor
Who is always a full hour late,
If I'm sure his waiting room magazines
Are all of the current date.

Charlotte weighed 285 pounds. One day she tripped on the stairs and broke her leg. The doctor put it in a cast and warned her that she wasn't to attempt going up or down stairs until it came off. Four months later he removed the cast and pronounced her well on the way to recovery.

"Oh, goody," gurgled Charlotte. "Is it all right for me to walk the stairs now?"

"Yes," said the M.D., "if you promise to be careful."

"I can't tell you what a relief it will be," confessed the woman. "It was such a nuisance crawling outside and shinnying up and down that drainpipe all the time!"

There is something ominous about the fact that doctors are usually described as practicing ...

Bronson rushed into a doctor's office.

"It's my wife," he gasped. "There's something very wrong with her. Her face seems to have frozen up, and she can't speak!"

"Hmmm ... It could be lockjaw," replied the physician.

"Could it really? In that case, doctor, if you happen to be in our neighborhood during the next few weeks, perhaps you could drop in and have a look at her . . ."

Telegram to famous physician:
MOTHER-IN-LAW AT DEATH'S DOOR.
CAN YOU PULL HER THROUGH?

Morse ignored the chiropractor's reputation for being rough and paid him a visit. By the time Morse left the office, he'd signed one check and two confessions.

"This may hurt a little," said the doctor as he stepped forward with the syringe.

Suddenly Mrs. Bingham let out an agonizing howl.

"What's the matter with you?" asked the M.D. "I haven't touched you yet."

"Not with the syringe, you haven't," said the woman, "but you're standing right on my corn."

Dr. Hogarth called the Texas oilman aside and said, "Shall I give your wife a local anesthetic?"

"No," snapped the Texan. "I'm rich, give her the best! Give her something imported!"

Brannigan was recovering nicely from an operation, but he hated breakfast. Every morning they brought him the same thing: A glass of apple juice, a soft-boiled egg, toast and coffee and a urinal bottle which they wanted him to fill up when he finished. One morning Brannigan was sick of the breakfast so he ate the egg, the toast, drank the coffee but he poured the apple juice into the urinal bottle.

Miss Foster, the "we" nurse, arrived and asked, "Did we enjoy breakfast?" Then looking at the bottle, she said, "We must have been a bad boy because this looks a little cloudy."

"Well, then we better run it through again!" said Brannigan, raising the bottle to his lips.

A prominent doctor has discovered that cheerful people resist disease better than chronic grumblers. His theory is that the surly bird catches the germ.

What is the difference between an itch and an allergy? About $25 a visit.

A rather pompous surgeon was in the middle of a long speech after a charity fund-raising dinner.

"Let it never be said," he intoned, "that our profession receives its full due in the eyes of society. Indeed, we have many critics in this world."

"Not to mention," whispered a lawyer, "those in the next."

"Cheer up!" said the doctor, "I have the same ailment as you."

"Yeah," said the lawyer, "but you don't have the same doctor."

Dr. Hanworth finished examining Logan and said, "Your heart is in bad shape. You need a transplant. It's very expensive."

"How much?" asked Logan.

"I've got a heart in the freezer of a 35-year-old man ... exercised a little, never ate fried foods. It'll cost $100,000."

"What else have you got?" asked the patient.

"You can have the heart of a 20-year-old decathlon runner. Never smoked or drank. He was in perfect physical condition. $200,000."

"Look, I'm only gonna do this once," said Logan. "What's the best you've got?"

"If you really want to go first class," said the M.D., "we've got the heart of a 65-year-old man. He drank two fifths of scotch every day. Smoked three packs of cigarettes. He was 50 pounds overweight. Had high cholesterol. It's $1,000,000."

"Wait a minute, why does this one cost so much more than all the others?"

"This is the heart of an attorney and it's never been used."

Legal Levity

Dr. Douglas telephoned his lawyer to discuss a malpractice insurance problem. "It's a big headache," said Bradford.

"I know," said the lawyer. "but it's late. Why don't you take two aspirin and call me in the morning?"

A physician and his wife were chatting over breakfast.

"I'm beginning to think our lawyer is only interested in how much money he can get out of me," said the M.D.

"Why do you say that?"

"He sent us a bill that said: 'For waking up at night and thinking about your case: $300.' "

Some doctors direct their patients to lie always on the right side, declaring that it is injurious to the health to lie on both sides. Yet, lawyers as a class enjoy good health.

Dr. Van Derber was fuming when he finally reached his table at a charity dinner. Van Derber explained to the lawyer seated next to him that a woman he'd just met kept badgering him for advice on a personal medical problem.

"I'd like to send her a bill," declared the doctor.

159

"Of course," replied the attorney. "You rendered professional services even if only informally."

"Thanks," said Van Derber, "I'll just do that."

The next day the doctor went to this office, prepared to send the annoying woman a bill. On his desk he found a letter from the lawyer: "For legal services, $100."

BUMPER STICKER
Help The Legal Profession—
Go Into Medicine

Dr. Klippert was driving down the foggy Oregon coast highway one night when he crashed into another car driven by Grayson, an attorney. It was hard to tell who was at fault. Both men were shaken up, and the lawyer offered some whiskey from a pocket flask.

Klippert took the flask with a shaking hand and took several long swallows. When Grayson started to cap the flask, the doctor said, "A stiff drink could help the nerves. Why don't you have one, also?"

"Oh, I will," replied the lawyer, "right after the police get here."

A potential client asked the lawyer, "And what is a contingency fee?"

"A contingency fee to a lawyer means if I don't win your suit I get nothing. If I do win it you get nothing."

First Lawyer: As soon as I realized it was a crooked business I got out of it.
Second Lawyer: How much?

Bryant thumped his crutch on the office floor as he confronted Ramsey his attorney. "Your bill is outrageous!" he exclaimed. "You're taking four-fifths of my damages. I never heard of such extortion."

"I furnished the skill, the eloquence and the necessary legal learning for your case," said Ramsey.

"Yes," said the client, "but I furnished the case itself."

"That's ridiculous!" sneered the lawyer. "Anybody could fall down a manhole!"

Did you hear about the lawyer who was hurt in an accident?

The ambulance backed up suddenly.

A cruise ship was wrecked in a storm. Next morning the survivors found themselves on a desert island without food or water. They noticed the wreckage of the ship on a sand bar only 500 yards from the shore but there were sharks swimming all around the inlet.

"I'll swim out and get food," volunteered a young man. "I used to be a life guard."

He dove into the water and in a few minutes was attacked and devoured by the sharks. Another man stepped forward. "I'm only a CPA, but I'm a strong swimmer. I can make it."

But he didn't. Forty yards off shore the sharks tore him apart. Suddenly up stepped a paunchy, bespectacled, bald-headed man. "I'm a lawyer and I think I can get to the ship."

He entered the water and immediately eight sharks formed a two-lane escort and helped him to the ship and back, unharmed.

"Good heavens!" shouted one of the passengers, "it's a miracle!"

"Miracle, hell!" said the lawyer. "It's just professional courtesy."

LAWYER
A fellow who is willing to go out
and spend your last cent
to prove he is right.

Roth rushed into court and asked that a new trial be granted his client who had been found guilty the day before. "I've uncovered new evidence," said the attorney.

"What kind?" asked the judge.

"My client has an extra $2,000 and I found out about it only this morning," replied Roth.

Conrad flew to Fort Worth to try an important case, promising to wire his partner the moment a decision was announced. At long last the wire came:

JUSTICE HAS TRIUMPHED

The partner in Chicago wired back:

APPEAL AT ONCE

"Here's my bill," said Prewitt. "Please give me $5,000 as a down payment and then $500 a month thereafter for twelve months."

"Sounds like buying an automobile," said the client.

"I am," returned the attorney.

Gassner, a young lawyer who had taken over his father's practice, rushed home one evening totally elated. "Dad, listen," he shouted. "I've settled that old Mead suit at last."

"*Settled it!*" cried the astonished parent. "Why I gave you that as an annuity for your life."

A lawyer is a man who prevents someone else from getting your money.

Hazlett had an important trial coming up so he went to the finest tailor in Atlanta and ordered a custom-made suit. When he arrived for the final fitting, Hazlett was delighted at the wonderful cut, the marvelous texture of the cloth and the magnificent styling. But when he went to put his money into the pockets Hazlett found there weren't any.

"But why no pockets?" he protested to the tailor.

"You don't need 'em," answered the tailor. "Who ever heard of a lawyer with his hands in his own pockets?"

Leaver and Coyle met at a cocktail party. "How's business?" asked Leaver.

"Rotten!" answered Coyle. "Yesterday I chased an ambulance 20 miles. When I caught up, there was another lawyer already in it."

Bernstein had been arrested for speeding, passing a red light, going through a stop sign, and driving without a license. He hired his nephew, just graduated from law school, and demanded a trial by jury.

"But you can't win in court," said his friend, Fishman.

"I know," said Bernstein, "but this is my nephew's first case and I want him to lose so he'll get an honest job."

Mrs. Silverstein, a wealthy old lady, sent for Levine to make out her will.

The lawyer was gentle and sympathetic. "Now don't you worry about this," he said to the ailing dowager, "just leave it all to me."

"I might as well," sighed the old woman, "you'll get it anyway."

WILL
A dead giveaway.

Jane and Debra were having cocktails. "Whatever is the matter?" asked Jane. "You're absolutely falling apart!"

"I can't help it," sobbed Debra. "Vern got so excited about reincarnation that he went to a lawyer and changed his will. He's leaving everything to himself!"

Hopkins, an elderly miser, lay on his deathbed. He had no friends so he summoned his doctor, lawyer, and minister to his bedside. "They say you can't take it with you, but I am going to prove you can," gasped the dying man. "I've got $600,000 in cash under my mattress. I want you each to take an envelope now and just before they shovel the dirt on me you throw the envelopes in."

The three attended the funeral and each threw in his envelope. On the way back from the cemetery, the minister said, "Gentlemen, I want to confess. I needed $50,000 badly for a new church building, so I took out $50,000 and threw only $150,000 in the grave."

"I gotta tell the truth, too!" said the doctor, "I'm building a hospital and took $100,000 and threw in only $100,000."

"Fellas," said the lawyer, "I'm shocked. Keeping that money was a shameful thing to do. I threw in my personal check for the full amount."

Ignorance of the law does not prevent the losing lawyer from collecting his bill.

"Before I take your case," said the counselor, "you'll have to give me a $200 retainer."

"All right, here's the two hundred," agreed Mercer, handing over the money.

"Thank you," he retorted. "This entitles you to two questions!"

"What! Two hundred bucks for just two questions! Isn't that awfully high?"

"Yes, I suppose it is," said the lawyer. "Now, what's your second question?"

LAWYER
A man who helps you get
what's coming to him.

Client: I know the evidence is strong against my innocence, but I have $50,000 to fight the case.
Lawyer: As your attorney, I assure you that you'll never go to prison with that amount of money.
And he didn't. He went in broke.

Two Dublin barristers were sipping some brew at a popular pub.

"Patrick's developin' quite a reputation!"

"That he is. Ever since three of his clients were hung he's known as 'Swing and Sway with Briefcase O'Shay.'"

Did you hear about the lawyer who was so successful he had his own ambulance?

Gomez, who shot a fellow in a barroom dispute, wired to Galveston for a lawyer to defend him. The answer came:
ARRIVING BY PLANE TOMORROW
BRINGING TWO EYE WITNESSES

Mrs. Axelrod and Mrs. Baum, two grandmothers, sat poolside at a posh Puerto Rican hotel and chatted about their children.

"My son is a lawyer!" bragged Mrs. Axelrod.

"Yeah?" said Mrs. Baum, "so, how's he doin'?"

"My son is so brilliant he could look at a contract and immediately tell you whether it's oral or written."

SOLICITOR'S SONG
She was only a lawyer's daughter,
But she went from bar to bar.

A Fresno lawyer was called in to see a man in the county jail accused of murder.

When he returned to his office, his young law clerk said, "Well, did you take the case, Mr. Allison?"

"No, I didn't."

"Why? Didn't you think the man was justified in his act?"

"My son," said the lawyer, "he certainly was not financially justified in committing murder."

Lawyers sometimes tell the truth—they will do anything to win a case.

Carlson and Speckles were chatting about their teenagers.

"And what's your boy going to do for a living?" asked Carlson.

"I'm gonna let him be a lawyer," said Speckles. "He's naturally argumentative and bent on mixing into other people's troubles so he might just as well get paid for his time."

Nugent needed legal advice, so he walked into the office of Gavin, Barrison and Gavin. Nugent sat down at the desk of the senior member of the firm.

"If you're not really in bad trouble, I'll take the case," said Gavin. "If you're in a real jam and want to get out of it, my partner will handle it. If, on the other hand, you're not involved and want to get in trouble, my son, who just graduated from law school, will take it!"

Newly was relaxing in his club. "Say, do you think it'll rain?" he asked Gates, a lawyer sitting next to him.

"I wouldn't say so," answered Gates. The next day Newly received a bill for legal advice.

A week later they met again at the club, and Newly casually said, "Think we're going to have war with Russia?"

"I doubt it," replied the lawyer.

The next day his bill arrived at Newly's home.

Newly took the second bill and rushed to the club. He found Gates relaxing in an armchair and stormed up to him.

"Listen, you shyster, you're a crook!" he shouted. "And remember, I'm not *asking*, I'm *telling*!"

The courtroom was packed. Attorney Barker raised his voice so everyone could hear plainly.

"Repeat the words the defendant used," said the lawyer.

"I'd rather not. They were not fit words to tell a gentleman."

"Then," said the attorney, "whisper them to the judge."

In Miami, Brotsky the butcher burst open the door marked *Private* and stood before Nyman the attorney.

"If a dog steals a piece of meat from my shop, is the owner liable?" he asked.

"Certainly," replied the lawyer.

"Okay, your dog took a piece of sirloin steak worth ten dollars about five minutes ago."

"That right?" said Nyman. "Then just give me another ten and that'll cover my fee."

Did you hear about the process server in San Francisco who's getting altogether too cocky to suit his cronies?

They don't like the way he's been putting on the writs.

An attorney is like a porcupine. It's impossible to touch him without pricking one's finger.

Ames had a lawsuit involving a property title. When he walked into the courtroom, Larker, his opponent, came over to him. "Are those your witnesses sitting over there?"

"They are," said Ames.

"Then you win," said the lawyer. "I've used those witnesses twice myself."

PERSISTENT LAWYER
One who wouldn't hesitate
to spend an entire evening
trying to break a girl's will.

A psychological test was prepared to see how members of different professions would answer the same question. An engineer and a lawyer were called in. The examiner asked the engineer, "How much is two times two?"

The engineer replied, "Three point nine, nine, nine, nine. . . ."

Then he asked the lawyer, "How much is two times two?"

The lawyer said, "How much do you want it to be?"

Some men inherit money
Some men earn it and
Some are lawyers.

Did you hear about the lawyer who was so smart he never bothered to graduate?

He settled out of class.

After a heated exchange during a trial, the judge asked both counselors to approach the bench.

"Your Honor," said the lawyer Brewster, "I objected because my distinguished colleague was badgering the witness. It's obvious he's never heard of the Bill of Rights."

"Ridiculous!" snapped attorney Friedman, "I happen to know them by heart."

"Oh, really?" said Brewster. "I've got a hundred bucks that says you can't even tell me the first few words."

"Okay, wiseguy!" charged Friedman. "I pledge allegiance to the flag . . ."

"Damn," interrupted Brewster, handing over the money. "I didn't think you'd know it."

Young Ellison had just moved into his new Century City office and was awaiting his first client. Suddenly he heard footsteps coming down the hall, heading for his office. Quickly, the new bar member sat down behind his desk, picked up the phone and began talking to nobody.

"Well," said Ellison, "I'm very busy right now and I've got to be in court this afternoon and the next day."

He looked up to see a man standing at the door watching, then continued his make-believe conversation to make certain he impressed the man.

"Perhaps," he said into the phone, "I can squeeze you in Tuesday afternoon. Good. See you then."

Ellison hung up the phone and turned to the man at the door. "Yes, can I be of some help?"

"No," came the reply, "I just came to connect your telephone."

When a student first enters law school he is provided with a huge book containing the subject to study. The table of contents reads like this:

| Page | 1–20 | Libel Law |
| Page | 21–25 | Divorce Law |

"Tell me," said the personnel director of a large corporation, "are you an honest attorney?"

"Honest?" Cox replied. "Let me tell you something. My father lent me twenty thousand dollars for my education, and I paid him back in full after my very first case."

"I'm impressed," he said. "And what case was that?"

"He sued me for the money."

What do you call 5000 lawyers at the bottom of the ocean?

A good start.

A lawyer will never admit that the person he's defending is guilty. More than likely this will be his defense:

"My client is alleged to have killed his wife. He is supposed to have chopped up her body into little pieces, and stuffed them into a suitcase. He was apprehended trying to cross the border into Mexico when someone noticed that a piece of a thumb was sticking out of the suitcase.

"Now ladies and gentlemen of the jury, I know what you're thinking. You think that my client is a beast, he's a killer, he's a maniac. Well, I don't see him that way. A sloppy packer, maybe . . ."

Talk's cheap—if lawyers don't do the talking.

One day the gate between Heaven and Hell broke down. St. Peter called out to the Devil. "Hey, Satan, it's your turn to fix it."

"Sorry," said the Devil. "My men are too busy shoveling coal. We can't worry about a mere gate."

"All right," declared St. Peter, "I'll have to sue you for breaking our agreement."

"Go ahead!" snapped Satan. "Where are you gonna get a lawyer?"

Fuller graduated from law school and was taken into his father's firm. "Any advice, Dad?" he asked.

"Yes, my boy. When fighting a case, it's always been my policy that if the law is on my side, I hammer on the law. If the facts are on my side, I hammer on the facts."

"But if you don't have the facts or the law?" asked Fuller.

"In that case, I hammer on the table."

Only lawyers can write documents containing 5,000 or more words and call it a brief.

The senior partner of a prestigious Pittsburgh law firm was speaking to the young wife of the company's newest partner.

"You know, Mrs. Baylock, your husband is an absolutely honest man. He seems passionately concerned with the attainment of justice."

"That's a wonderful quality," said the wife.

"Yes," said the boss, "if only he wasn't a lawyer."

The defendant in a Jersey City court sent a note to the judge, while his long-winded lawyer continued to orate. "If I should be found guilty," he wrote, "would the Court please credit my sentence with all the time taken up by my lawyer?"

During the early days of the United States Supreme Court, there were some pretty heavy drinkers. A rule was finally adopted among them to drink alcohol only when the weather was inclement, raining or snowing.

The next week, one of the jurists staggered into the chambers three sheets to the wind.

"Didn't we agree that there would be drinking only during inclement weather?"

"Yes, but we as a supreme court represent the whole United States. Surely it must be raining or snowing some place in this country."

A lawyer said to a friend, "I want you to be a witness in an accident case."

"Okay, but I'll tell you now, I haven't got time to come to the rehearsals."

Abraham Lincoln was involved in a case to be heard in the local courthouse so he sought out the town tavern the evening before. When Abe reached the inn, the huge fireplace in the sitting room was surrounded by all the other lawyers interested in the case.

"Really cold out, eh?" asked the innkeeper.

"Colder than hell," answered Lincoln.

"You've been there, too, Mr. Lincoln?" asked a bystander.

"Oh, yes," smiled Abe, "and it's just as it is here. All the lawyers are nearest the fire."

Miss Nelson heard one of her pupils crying and rushed out to the playground.

"What is the trouble?" she asked of little Cliff, who was eating an apple.

"Burl took Rod's apple," explained the witness.

"And where is the apple?" asked the teacher.

"I've got that," replied Cliff. "You see, I'm the lawyer."

The law presumes a man innocent until he is found guilty, and then if he has any money left, his lawyer continues the presumption.

A young lawyer from the North sought to locate in the South. He wrote to a friend in Mississippi, asking him what the prospects seemed to be in the city for "an honest young lawyer and Republican."

The friend wrote back: "If you are an honest lawyer, you will have absolutely no competition. If you are a Republican, the game laws will protect you."

BUMPER STICKER
Honk If You've Never Been
Cheated By A Lawyer

Thatcher, in a state of hysteria, went to an attorney. "What am I going to do?" he asked. "Dinelli is suing me for breaking an irreplaceable antique plate of his!"

"Don't worry," said the lawyer. "We have at least three lines of defense. In the first place, we will prove that you never borrowed the plate from Dinelli. In the second place, we'll prove that when you borrowed the plate it was already damaged beyond repair. And in the third place, we'll prove that when you returned it, it was in absolutely perfect condition."

What's brown and black and looks good on a lawyer?
A doberman.

A Chicago woman in desperate trouble persuaded the great Clarence Darrow to handle her litigation. The lawyer defended her brilliantly and won her case in a breeze.

When it was all over, she said to him, "Oh, Mr. Darrow, how can I ever show my appreciation?"

"My dear woman," responded Darrow, "ever since the Phoenicians invented money, there has been only one answer to that question."

Recently, a man in Albuquerque left the bulk of his fortune to his lawyer. If everybody did this, a lot of time would be saved.

When the American Bar Association held its convention in San Francisco, it was attended by over 12,000 lawyers. The day they arrived, every burglar alarm in town went off.

Did you hear about the Texas lawyer who got his client a suspended sentence?
They hung him.

Updyne was spending the summer in a tiny New Hampshire town. One morning he approached Gavin, a weather-beaten old timer. "Excuse me," said Updyne, "are you a resident here?"

"Yeah," said the senior citizen. "I've lived in this town goin' on fifty years. What kin I do for you?"

"I am looking for a criminal lawyer," said the visitor. "Have you any here?"

"Well," said the old man, "we're pretty sure we have, but we can't prove it."

Fowler took his dog to the Langley Obedience School. "You can have your dog trained to do anything," said Langley. "Even to learn your trade."

"What do you mean?" asked Fowler.

Langley took a bunch of bones, dropped them on the ground and whistled for a dog. The animal trotted out, grabbed the bones and in a few moments had built a house.

"Now that dog belongs to an architect," announced the dog trainer.

"Amazing!" said Fowler.

Langley dismantled the bones, threw them on the ground and released another dog. This time the canine built a skeleton. "He's owned by a doctor!" said Langley.

"That's incredible," blurted Fowler.

Suddenly, a third dog wandered out. This one ate all the bones and then peed on both dogs.

"Good heavens!" shouted Fowler. "Who owns that one?"

"Oh, that dog belongs to a divorce lawyer!"

Golfer Guffaws

"Golf sure is a stupid game!"

"You're absolutely right! I'm glad I don't have to play again until tomorrow."

Kiernan was lining up his putt on the eight green when suddenly a woman dressed in a bridal gown came running toward him.

"This is our wedding day," she shouted. "How could you do this to me?"

"Listen, Joyce," said Kiernan, "I told you only if it's raining. *Only* if it's raining!"

Did you hear the one about the Siamese twins who walked up to the starter's window and asked. "Do you have a tee for two?"

GOLFER
One who can tote 25 pounds
of equipment several miles,
but needs Junior to bring him
the ash tray.

A stranger joined a threesome on a public course on the first tee. "What do you shoot?" they asked.

"78!" he replied.

On the first hole he got a seven. On the second hole he got a six. When they got to the twelfth hole, he picked up his ball and said, "So long, fellas, I got my 78!"

Kenyon: How come you're so late?
Rooney: I had to toss a coin between church and golf.
Kenyon: Then why are you so late?
Rooney: I had to toss seventeen times!

Wayne and Vic were playing a mountainous course in the Swiss Alps. Wayne rejoined his partner after playing a difficult lie at the bottom of a crevasse.

"How many?" asked Vic.

"Three."

"Three? I heard six!"

"Three were echoes."

"That man cheats," cried Washburn as he entered the clubhouse. "He lost his ball in the rough and played another ball without losing a stroke."

"How do you know he didn't find his ball?" asked a friend.

"Because I've got it in my pocket."

"Why do you love golf so much?"

"It makes me forget whom I work for and who I'm married to."

Victor had been marooned on a desert island for more than twelve years when one day a beautiful blonde in a wet suit swam up on the beach. Victor greeted her excitedly and complained about missing the civilized conveniences.

"Would you like a cigarette?" asked the blonde beauty.

"Yes, of course."

The girl reached inside her wet suit and provided the smokes. Then she asked, "Would you like a drink?"

"Oh, Lord! Please!"

She reached inside her wet suit and handed over a bottle.

Between sips Victor gasped, "God, this is great! You're the first woman I've seen in over twelve years!"

"Well," said the blonde starting to unzip her wet suit, "would you like to play around?"

"Wow! Don't tell me you've got a set of golf clubs in there?"

"I suppose you heard that Ernie killed his wife?"

"Really, how?"

"With a 4-iron!"

"Oh? How many strokes?"

Darnell and Corbett were having a neighborly chat when a funeral procession went by. In the lead car, instead of flowers there were golf clubs. Nothing but golf clubs in a top grain leather bag.

"That's what I call a real tribute to a golfer," said Darnell. "They're gonna bury the clubs right with him. He must have really loved the game!"

"He still loves the game," said Corbett. "It's his wife that died. Right after the funeral it's back to the golf course!"

Did you hear about the rich Texan who hired a full-time caddy for his electric putting machine?

GOLFERS ANONYMOUS
When you get the urge to play golf,
they send someone over to drink with
you till the urge passes.

"Eugene, you promised to be home at two o'clock this afternoon and now it's after six."

"Honey, please! My best friend Wally is dead—dropped dead on the 10th green this morning."

"Oh, how terrible."

"It certainly was. The whole day, it's been hit the ball ... drag Wally ... hit the ball ... drag Wally ..."

Wife: I know it's too much to expect, but if you ever spent a Sunday with me, instead of on the golf course, I think I'd drop dead.

Husband: It'll do no good to try to bribe me.

One midsummer morning Evan announced to his wife at breakfast, "It's too nice a day to go to the office."

"Good," said the wife, "but don't think you're going to play golf. There are a lot of things that need doing around the house."

"Golf was the farthest thing from my mind," protested Evan. "Now, would you mind passing the putter?"

"My wife says if I don't give up golf, she'll leave me."

"Wow! What tough luck."

"Yeah! I'm gonna miss her."

Golfer: Pardon, but would you mind letting me play through? My wife just had a serious operation and I've got to get to the hospital as quickly as I can!

Two Chicago yuppies, Crawford and Webb, flew to Hawaii for a week of golf. They agreed that the loser would pick up the entire tab for the trip.

On the last day of their vacation, Crawford led Webb by only two strokes, but still had to sink a 40-foot putt on the

18th hole. As he started to putt, a mangy-looking dog suddenly trotted out across the green between the ball and the hole. Without blinking, Crawford stroked the ball smoothly and sent it in a graceful arc directly into the cup.

"Wow!" cried Webb. "That was the greatest display of coolness I've ever seen on a golf course."

"What do you mean?"

"The way you didn't move a muscle when that dog ran in front of you."

"What dog?"

Wakefield and Vernon were watching a hearse lead a line of cars through a cemetery gate.

"Isn't that a shame," said Wakefield. "That fella was practicing with a 5-iron in his backyard and he knocked the ball through the kitchen window and killed his wife!"

"How do you like that?" said Vernon. "I have trouble with my 5-iron too!"

Kirk and Lloyd had just landed on the 12th green of their club course when a funeral procession slowly wound its way past them on the adjoining highway.

Kirk doffed his cap and bowed his head low until the cortege disappeared.

"That was a nice gesture," said Lloyd. "I had no idea you were so sentimental."

"It was the least I could do," replied Kirk. "Two more days and we would have been married 25 years!"

GOLF
The game that has turned the cows
out of the pasture and let the bull in.

Jim and Ethel, married 23 years, were having a heated argument.

"You're always talking about golf! Golf! Golf!" she screeched. "You can't even remember what day we got married."

"Sure I do," yawned Jim, "it was the day after I sank that 30-foot putt on the 16th hole."

Did you hear about the golfer who was so used to cheating that when he got a hole-in-one he put down a zero on his score card?

"Good Lord! I think your partner is having a stroke!"
"Just so he doesn't get it on our scorecard!"

Mr. and Mrs. Belden were playing a course way out in the country. On the 14th hole he hit a ball that landed behind a barn. "I'll pick it up and take a stroke!" said Belden.

"Don't be silly," said his spouse. "I'll open the back door of the barn and then the front—you could hit the ball straight through!"

He agreed. She opened the doors. He sliced the ball. It hit the barn, bounced off his wife's skull and killed her instantly.

One year later, Belden was playing with a friend and his ball landed near the same spot. Again, he offered to pick it up and take a stroke penalty.

"Hey," said his partner, "I'll open the barn doors—you could hit the ball straight through."

"No, thanks!" said Belden. "I had the same lie last year, and it cost me three strokes!"

Husband: Sweetheart, I have a present for the person I love best in all the world.
Wife: A set of golf clubs, no doubt.

Grubbs played golf every weekend with the same friend. One Saturday he was sitting around the house reading. "Sweetheart," said his wife, "aren't you playing golf today with George?"

"Absolutely not. Would you play golf with a man who lies, cheats and moves his ball?"

"No!"

"Neither will George!"

Three drunks were stumbling down the third fairway on a course near the Everglades in Florida. The one leading the group walked into some quicksand and slowly began to sink. Soon only his right arm was sticking out.

"Look," said one of the other drunks, "he wants the 5-iron!"

GOLF
A game in which a little white ball
is chased by a lot of gaffers
too old to chase anything else.

Erlen and Varney were getting ready to tee off when they noticed a funeral up at the top of the ridge.

"Look, they're burying Harry!"

"Too bad, eh?"

"What's even worse, look where they're burying him! You know how Harry hated a downhill lie!"

Wright was keeping an eagle eye on his opponent in the rough when he returned to the fairway and asked, "How do you lie, three?"

"No, just two," he answered. "That was a practice swing I took over there."

"Okay," said Wright, "but you're the first person I ever heard curse after a practice swing."

Wheeler and Pierce, two bitter rivals who didn't trust each other's arithmetic, were playing a heated match—and watching each other like hawks.

After holing out on the fourth green and marking his own six on the scorecard, Wheeler asked his opponent what he had had.

Pierce went through the motions of mentally counting up. "Six!" he said and then hastily corrected himself. "No—a five."

Calmly Wheeler marked the scorecard uttering, "Eight."

"Eight? I couldn't have had eight."

"No. You claimed six, then changed it to five. But actually you had a seven."

"Then why mark down an eight?"

"One stroke penalty," said Wheeler, "for improving your lie."

"If I were you, I'd play golf for my health."

"But I do play golf, doctor."

"In that case, I'd quit."

A pro, hired by a big department store to give lessons, was approached by two women.

"Do you want to learn to play golf, ma'am?" he asked one.

"No, no," she said. "It's my friend who wants to learn. I learned yesterday."

Irma and Jean, two slightly overweight beginners, waddled out to the first tee of the Cleveland golf course one morning.

"I don't want to play too long," said Irma after she teed off.

"Me neither," said Jean. "Let's quit as soon as either of us makes a hole in one!"

"Caddy, why do you keep looking at your watch?"

"This isn't a watch, sir, it's a compass."

Alice and Dora were approaching the 10th tee. A foursome about to hit suggested that the ladies play through.

"Thank you, gentlemen," said Alice. Then, to her partner, "Go ahead, Dora, you're up!"

"I am not. You have the honors."

"No, I don't, Dora. I had a 14."

The president of the local women's club was telling her husband of their plans to raise money for the club.

"We're going to serve as Caddies-For-A-Day at the Country Club, but don't know what to call ourselves. We've thought of Caddy-ettes and Links Lassies, but we need something more original."

"I have it," offered her husband. "How about Tee Bags?"

Wife: Vincent our son says he caddied for you this afternoon.

Husband: Funny, I knew I'd seen that damn kid before.

"I suppose you've seen worse golfers in your time, caddy?"

No reply.

"I said, I suppose you've seen worse golfers in your time?"

"I heard you the first time, sir. I'm just trying to remember."

Golfer: Watch my swing. I don't think I'm playing my usual game.

Caddy: What game is that, sir?

At a water hole, Kendrick asked his caddy for a 5-iron. "Bet you a hundred you can't get over the water with a 5!" challenged his partner.

"You got a bet!" said Kendrick.

"Hey," said one of the fellows in the foursome, "can we get in on this?"

"Sure!" said Kendrick. "I'll bet you both a hundred bucks I can clear this water with my 5-iron!"

Kendrick walked up to the ball. "Double or nothing on the caddy fees?" asked his caddy.

"Sure," said Kendrick, "might as well take your money too!"

Then he approached the ball, took a practice swing, looked at the water and then said, "Caddy, you better give me an old ball!"

Neil and Ward were discussing the golfing prowess of the men they had carried for that day.

Neil said, "My guy had a ten on the first hole. Then an 8, then a 10, then a 7, then another 10—and then he blew up!"

Probably the original caddy joke is this one straight from Scotland:

"Caddy, are you good at finding balls?"

"Yes, sir!"

"Well, go out and find one now and we'll start."

Scotsman: I lost a brand new ball today.
Englishman: Oh, did the string break?

Adam and Cal were on the third tee, feeling a little bit guilty about golfing on Sunday morning.

"I suppose we shouldn't be playing today," said Adam. "We should've gone to church."

"I couldn't have gone to church this morning anyway," replied Cal. "The wife is very sick!"

GOLF BALL
A small, indented object which
remains on the tee while a perspiring
human fans it vigorously
with a large club.

The minister and his sexton played golf together regularly, despite the sexton's winning with monotonous regularity.

One day after he'd won by a large, lopsided score, the sexton sought to lighten the defeat, saying, "Don't worry, Parson, you'll get ahead of me in the end when you read the burial service over my grave."

"No," said the clergyman, "I think that will be your hole, too."

Reverend Burkett had given up golf for Lent. But one day, driving by his favorite course, he found the temptation too much and soon he was teeing off and headed for the fifth hole.

From heaven, Gabriel spotted him and reported to God.

"Disgusting, isn't it, Boss?" said the angel.

"Yes, he must be punished, but watch him play this next hole. I've arranged a little something."

The minister teed up on a 560-yard hole, hit a terrific drive that sailed out 300 yards, bounced off a rock for another 100 yards, hit a tree and rebounded straight onto the green and rolled into the cup.

"Hey, God! That's how You punish him for breaking his Lenten promise? A 560-yard hole-in-one?"

"That's his punishment," said the Lord. "The greatest golf shot in history . . . and he can't tell anybody about it."

"Why do you play golf?"

"To aggravate myself."

Reverend Radburn was invited to play with Peyton, one of his parishioners. As Peyton squared up to the ball, he joked to the Reverend, "I think I'll offer up a prayer while I hit the ball."

He took a big swing and completely missed the ball.

"Well," said Peyton, "I guess that prayer didn't do much good, eh?"

"No," said the minister, "but next time try keeping your head down when you pray."

Denahy was not much of a churchgoer for he played with the same foursome every Sunday. Father Flynn, the parish priest, admonished him.

"Father," murmured Denahy, "I just want to know if there are any golf courses in heaven."

"I don't know," replied the priest. "I'll check with the Pope."

The next day Father Flynn reported to Denahy, "My son, I've got good news and bad news. Here's the good news. There are plenty of courses in heaven. Beautiful fairways, greens smooth as silk. And it never gets dark, so you can play 24 hours a day."

"What's the bad news?" asked Denahy.

"Your tee off time is tomorrow morning at 8:10!"

"What's your handicap?"

"I'm too honest!"

Reardon, playing with Father Fallon, was badly off his game. Each time he missed the drive or putt, he muttered, "Dammit, I missed."

"My son," said Father Fallon, "should you continue to

use foul language, the heavens may open up and the good Lord may strike you down with a thunderbolt."

Reardon tried to control himself but when he shanked his next shot, he shouted, "Dammit, I missed!" At once the heavens opened, lightning ripped through the atmosphere and struck Father Fallon dead.

And from the heavens came a mighty voice, "Dammit, I missed!"

Sunday School

Teacher:	Jeremiah, do you know what becomes of boys who use bad language when they're playing marbles?
Jeremiah:	Yes, ma'am. They grow up and play golf.

Harrison played with Reverend Lambert, the minister of his church, once or twice a month.

Harrison had a habit of cursing the ball, the green, everything in sight. With Reverend Lambert, he held back, but by the end of the round he would be white with frustration.

Whenever the minister fumbled shots, he simply turned his head away.

"Reverend Lambert, how is it you keep your temper when you slice into the rough or you miss your putt?" asked Harrison.

"By sublimation," said the clergyman. "I don't shout or use vile language. That won't help and could imperil my soul. Since I must do something, I spit!"

"You spit?"

"Yes," replied the Reverend. "But where I spit, the grass never grows again!"

"Okay, so you got a hole-in-one on the first green. Now what's the bad news?"

"I shot 138 on the other 17."

OVERHEARD AT A PALM SPRINGS BAR

"You know, the closest I ever came to a hole-in-one was 13."

"Is Roger a bad golfer?"

"Bad? He's the only guy in the world who has an unplayable lie when he tees up!"

Have you heard about the new golf course for grass smokers?

POT and PUTT.

"Tell me, Reverend, is it a sin for me to play golf on Sunday?"

"I've seen you on the course, my son, and it's a sin for you to play any day of the week."

A game of golf's like taxes
        Both try a strong man's soul
    Drive hard to get up the green
        Then wind up in the hole.

Slow, elderly golfer: Let me tell you, young fella, that I was playing this game before you were born.

Impatient opponent: Well, would you mind trying to finish it before I die?

Did you hear about the Arab oil billionaire who bought his son a set of fourteen golf clubs?

All but one came with a swimming pool.

There was a young man called Hood
Who always sliced with a wood.
    One day he turned lefty

And hit 'em quite hefty
Now he's hooking his slice but good!

"What made you put off your wedding for two more days?"

"I figured out that my silver wedding anniversary would come out on a Saturday and I always play golf on Saturday."

HANDICAPPED GOLFER
A man who plays with his boss.

Bob Hope treated a Tonight Show audience to this tall tale about meeting Charlie Boswell, the blind golfer:

"I'll be happy to play a round with you," said Hope. "And if you like we can even make a small wager."

"Fine," said the golfer. "I'll bet you a $100 Nassau."

"Okay," said Hope. "What time do we tee off?"

"Two o'clock in the morning!" said the blind golfer.

"How did you do today."

"Well, I shot 9 on the first hole, 12 on the second, 16 on the third," piped the duffer, "but I blew it all on the fourth!"

Jess Oppenheimer, one of Hollywood's most gifted creators of comedy, has been telling this true story on himself for years. It seems Jess received a gift of several dozen golf balls with his name imprinted on them.

One day Jess hit a long drive off the tee onto the other fairway. As he strolled over to his ball he saw a player coming the other way about to hit it.

"Hold it!" said Jess nicely, "I think that's my ball!"

"No," said the man adamantly, "I've already checked."

"I think you'd better look again," advised Jess. "That happens to be my ball!"

"Not possible," exclaimed the other man, "I always play an Oppenheimer!"

Two psychiatrists were on the first green. The first one missed a two footer, and muttered, "Nuts!"

"Please, Max," said his partner, "let's not talk shop!"

Did you hear about the absent-minded dentist who, after lining up a six-foot putt, stared at the hole and said, "Open a little wider, please?"

A golfer had a terrible day on the links. At the last hole, he fell into a tantrum. Cursing and swearing, he beat on the ground with his 8-iron. "I have to give it up," he moaned. "I have to give it up."

"Give up golf?" asked his caddy.

"No," snapped the golfer, "the ministry."

Parson Prentice sauntered into his golf club one weekday morning. He wanted to play a round, but nobody familiar was in sight. The only other person in the locker room was a stranger.

The clergyman approached him and said, "Are you looking for a game?"

"Yes. I'd be glad to play with you. But I always play for $20 a round."

Prentice, even though he wasn't much of a golfer, was willing to pay $20 for the morning's pleasure, so he agreed.

Out on the links, the stranger took every unfair advantage. When the parson was putting, he'd start to jabber away. He cheated whenever he could, and he made the day miserable.

After Prentice had paid off, he said, "Come to my church

on Sunday. And you might bring along your parents, too. I'd like to meet them."

"Bring my mother and father? Why?"

"Because then," retorted the parson, "I could marry them."

Four-legged Fables

Gilman was more than a little annoyed when a neighbor telephoned at 3 a.m. and complained, "Your damn dog is barking so loud I can't sleep." The neighbor hung up before he could protest.

The following morning at 3 a.m., Gilman called his neighbor and said, "I don't have a dog."

Cameron walked into a department store and asked the security guard to hold his dog for a minute. When he returned the guard was kicking the poor little pup.

"Why are you kicking that defenseless dog?" asked Cameron.

"Why shouldn't I," said the guard, "he lifted up his leg like he was going to kick me!"

Morton stopped Barrett on Main Street.

"Your dog bit me," said Morton, "and I'm gonna sue."

"Tell you what," said Barrett, "I'll give you $100 to settle out of court."

"I'll take it. Say, what are you laughing at?"

"That's a counterfeit bill. What are you laughing at?"
"I've got a wooden leg."

"Do you know that your dog barked all night?"
"Yes, but don't worry. He sleeps all day."

A great big sheep dog was sent to a kennel, where his owners hoped he might learn to stop jumping on everybody who came into their home. At the kennel he got into a conversation with a tiny French poodle. "My name is Josette," said the little dog, "what's yours?"

"I'm not sure," said the sheep dog, "but I think it's Downboy."

Did you hear about the dog in San Francisco who just loves to be scrubbed three times a day?

His owners aren't sure of his breed, but they think he's a shampoodle.

A drunk was passing a bus intersection when a large St. Bernard brushed against him and knocked him down. An instant later a foreign sports car skidded around the corner and inflicted more damage.

A bystander helped the poor drunk up and said, "Are you hurt?"

"Well," he answered, "the dog didn't hurt so much, but that tin can tied to his tail nearly killed me."

"It's raining cats and dogs outside."
"I know. I just stepped in a poodle."

"My home town is so small our fire department consists of a hose, cart and four dogs."
"What do the dogs do, haul the cart?"
"No. They find the hydrant."

Sommers was walking down the main street of a small town, with a dog on a leash. The animal was a miserable-looking, mangy, flea-ridden, purple-eyed pup.

"Where are you going with that mutt?" asked a friend.

"Oh, I'm taking him to the New York Dog Show."

"That flea-bitten, raggedy-looking character? You'll never win a prize with him!"

"Yes, I know," he replied, "but it'll give him a chance to meet a lot of real nice dogs."

"Did you say your dog's bark was worse than his bite?" Norman asked a neighbor.

"Yes," said the fellow.

"Then for God's sake don't let him bark! He just bit half my pants off!"

Gaylord, age 72, was called before an Alabama judge and charged with keeping a vicious dog.

"That dog bit my girl Opal June three times," complained the mother.

"Did your dog bite little Opal June?" asked the judge.

"No suh," said Gaylord. "My dog, he never bit any little girl."

"Well," said the judge to the mother, "this man says the dog didn't bite your little girl."

"I'll go home and bring Opal June here and show you," said the woman.

"Hold on," said Gaylord. "In the first place the dog is so old he ain't got no teeth and he can't bite. In the second place the dog is blind and couldn't see Opal June anyhow. In the third place the dog is deaf and can't hear a thing, and in the fourth place he ain't my dog in the first place."

CANINE NATIONAL ANTHEM
My Country 'Tis A Tree

"Do you know that your dog bit my mother-in-law yesterday?"

"Is that so? Well, I suppose you'll sue me for damages?"

"Not at all. What'll you take for the dog?"

"I went hunting the other day," said Pearson, "and the dogs got in the way of a skunk. They finally gave up the chase."

"Did they lose the scent?" asked his neighbor.

"They gave up the skunk, but I don't think they'll ever lose the scent."

Norton, a New Yorker, went to the country for the first time to do some hunting. Carney, a kennel owner, provided the dogs to accompany Norton. The hunter left early the next morning but returned in an hour.

"Why are you back so soon?" asked Carney.

"I'm after more dogs."

"More dogs!" exclaimed the kennel owner. "Those were good dogs I gave you."

"I know, but I've shot those dogs already."

"Look here, don't you know my office hours are from 8 to 10?"

"Yes, doctor, but the dog that bit me didn't."

Harris took his dog to the veterinarian and asked him to cut his tail off completely.

"Why in the world would you want me to do that?" asked the vet.

"Well," said the dog owner, "my mother-in-law is coming to visit us, and I don't want anything in the house to suggest that she is welcome."

AFTER ONE YEAR OF MARITAL BLISS

She: Whenever I talk to you, it's like a dog barking. You never answer me.

He: It's not true! When's the last time you barked and I didn't answer?

Denton wanted to sell his Doberman, so he asked the local pet shop owner to look at the animal.

"This is a good dog," said Denton. "It cost me $1,000, but I'll let you have it for only $50."

"That's a rather big reduction," said the pet shop owner. "Is there something wrong with it?"

"No," said the man. "The fact is it turned on my wife one day and killed her, and now I've got no further use for it."

The famous rock and roll star was constantly stopped on the street by fans. Swooning girls would kiss his hand and tear pieces of clothes from his body. They even begged for locks of his hair which he agreed to send in the mail. And did.

One day a friend said, "You keep this up and you're gonna go bald in no time."

"Not me," he answered with a wink. "My dog!"

"My dog may not be pedigreed and all that, but he's a hell of a watch dog. No stranger ever gets anywhere near our house without our Buck letting us know."

"What does he do? You mean he growls and bites?"

"No—he crawls under our bed."

Ferris stormed out into Porter's Pet Shop. "I thought you said this dog was a good watchdog!" shouted Ferris.

"You mean he isn't?" asked Porter.

"No! Last night he barked so loud some burglars broke in, robbed us and left, and we didn't even hear them!"

As Hotchkiss drove along a seldom-traveled back road, a golden retriever ran out into the path of the car and was killed instantly.

Hotchkiss went to a nearby house. A woman was hanging clothes on a line so he explained what happened.

"It's my husband's dog," said the woman, "and he loved that dog a lot. Best hunting dog a man ever had."

"Well," said Hotchkiss, "where is your husband? I think I should tell him about it."

"He's back at the house, chopping wood," she replied. "But I don't want you to shock him what with his bad heart and all. So don't tell him it was the dog right off. Tell him it was me."

"Does your wife know how to take care of dogs?"
"Well, *I* look pretty healthy, don't I?"

A deaf man visited his friend and the dog barked at him like mad. Being unable to hear anything, he said to his friend after they had exchanged greetings, "Your dog didn't sleep well last night."

"Why do you say that?"

"He looked at me and kept yawning."

New Yorker Phelan, was visiting friends in Georgia. One day while out walking he came upon an old cracker dog, sitting in front of a cabin howling his head off. Phelan asked the animal's owner why he was howling.

"He's lazy," said the native.

"But," said the New Yorker, "is laziness painful?"

"Nope," said the Southerner.

"Then why does the dog howl?"

"Wal," said the Georgian, "that blame fool dawg is settin' on a sandburr, an' he's too tarnation lazy to git off. So he jes' sets there an' howls 'cause it hurts."

"What kind of an invention are you working on these days, Willie?"

"You can laugh. I know my other ideas didn't work out, but this time I got a winner."

"Really? What've you got?"

"I just invented a dog food that tastes like a mailman's ankle."

"I'm a little worried about our mailman."

"Why?"

"Last week I found a pile of bones on the front walk and our dog was picking his teeth with a postcard."

A South Dakota mailman complained to his boss that a dog had bitten him on the leg that morning. "Did you put anything on it?" asked his superior.

"No," replied the mail carrier. "He liked it just as it was."

CANINE CANTATA

A hungry dog went walking into a grocery store
The grocer tossed a frankfurter to Fido on the floor
He said, "Now, doggie, eat it." Said Fido, "I decline,
For in that sausage is an old sweetheart of mine."

McCreery had been bitten by a dog, and the wound was taking a long time to heal. Finally he consulted a doctor, who took one look and ordered the dog brought in.

The M.D. discovered that the dog had rabies. Since it was too late to give the patient a serum, the medico felt he had to prepare him for the worst. At that moment, McCreery sat down at the doctor's desk and began to write.

"Perhaps it won't be so bad," said the physician. "You needn't make out your will right now."

"I'm not making out any will," said the man. "I'm just writing out a list of people I'm going to bite."

Why are the dogs in Siberia the fastest in the world?
Because the trees are so far apart.

"Herb loves his dog so much, the mutt sleeps in the same bed with him."

"Really?"

"It isn't healthy, of course, but the dog has gotten used to it."

Felicia, a yuppie wife, was very fond of her pet, Buttons. One day, the dog ran out into the street and was killed by a passing car. She was in tears that night when her husband got home. His efforts to comfort her were to no avail.

Finally, he said, "Darling, stop crying and I'll buy you a new hat."

"But," she cried, "if you knew how much I miss him you'd make that a fur coat."

Wife: Why can't we live peacefully like the cat and dog lying side by side there at the fireplace. They never fight.

Husband: Yeah, but tie them together and then see what happens.

Did you hear about the dog who went to the flea circus and stole the whole show?

A well-meaning lady held a cookie above a dog and commanded, "Speak! Speak!"

"Why," said the dog modestly, "I hardly know what to say!"

Meeting in Central Park, a huge boxer stopped and wagged his tail in friendly greeting to a Russian wolfhound.

"How do you like America?" he asked.

"Well, it's different from my homeland," said the wolfhound. "In Russia I eat bones dipped in vodka and caviar. In Russia I have my own doghouse made of rare Siberian wood. In Russia I sleep on a rug made of thick warm ermine."

"Then why did you come to America?"

"I like to bark once in a while."

A dog had such a high I.Q. that his owner sent him to college. Home for Christmas, the dog admitted he hadn't learned any history or economics. "But," he said, "I did make a good start in foreign languages."

"Okay," said the owner, "say something in a foreign language."

The dog said, "Meow!"

Farrell, an antique dealer, noticed a mangy little kitten lapping up milk from a saucer in front of Drabinsky's Delicatessen. He recognized the saucer as being a rare and precious piece of pottery.

Just then Drabinsky came out. Farrell offered five dollars for the cat.

"It's not for sale," said Drabinsky.

"Look," said the antique connoisseur, "that cat is dirty and undesirable, but I'm eccentric. I like cats that way. I'll give you ten dollars."

"It's a deal," said the deli owner.

"For that much money I'm sure you won't mind throwing in the saucer," said Farrell. "The kitten seems so happy drinking from it."

"Nothing doing," said Drabinsky. "That's my lucky saucer. From that saucer, so far this week, I've sold thirty-eight cats."

"I heard you have a cat that can say her own name."
"That's right."
"What's her name?"
"Meow!"

CAT
An animal that never cries
over spilled milk

Kendrick met Grimes at the supermarket.
"Hey," said Kendrick, "remember that $5 check you gave me for drowning your cat?"
"Yeah," replied Grimes, "what about it?"
"It came back."
"So did the cat."

Did you hear about the pet shop owner who went crazy trying to take an inventory of the rabbits?

Ned and Brad, two high school seniors, were having a Coke. "Your grandfather's a little deaf, isn't he?" asked Ned.
"A *little* deaf?" replied Brad. "Yesterday he said his prayers kneeling on the cat!"

Jack: Didn't you know that black cats are unlucky?
Mack: This one isn't. He just ate your dinner.

The butcher was busy waiting on a woman when Mrs. Thompson rushed in and said, "Give me a pound of cat food, quick!"

Turning to the other customer, who had been waiting for some time, Mrs. Thompson said, "I hope you don't mind my getting waited on before you."

"Not if you're *that* hungry," replied the other woman.

There once were two cats in Kilkenny.
Each thought there was one cat too many.
And they scratched and they fit
And they tore and they bit.
'Till instead of two cats, there weren't any.

Stories about Yogi Berra's antics while a member of the New York Yankees are legion. This one is sworn to by a couple of Yogi's teammates.

One night the stocky catcher was horrified to see a small kitten toppling from the branches of a tree across the way from him. He dashed over and made a miraculous catch—but the force of habit proved too much for him. He straightened up and threw the cat to second base.

"Is it really bad luck to have a black cat cross your path?"

"Well, it depends on whether you're a man or a mouse."

The wealthy tourist lost his prized blue-eyed white Persian while stopping over in a tiny Southern town. He quickly inserted an ad in the local newspaper offering a $1000 reward.

The next day he dialed the newspaper office to inquire, but found no one there but the old janitor.

"Where's the newspaper staff?" asked the man.

"They all out," said the janitor, "tryin' ta find that cat of yours."

Linwood inserted a classified ad in a local newspaper offering a $500 reward for the return—no questions asked—of his wife's pet cat.

"That's a mighty big reward for a cat," said the clerk accepting the ad.

"Not for this one," said Linwood. "I drowned it."

CATASTROPHE
Top prize for the cat
with the most beautiful behind.

Neal, a student at Boston College, received a telephone call from his brother Marc back home.

"Hi, Neal," said Marc. "Your cat's dead."

Neal fell apart. He began crying uncontrollably. When, finally, he was able to compose himself, he scolded his brother.

"Dammit, Marc," he told him. "You know how I loved that cat. You didn't have to call me and just spill it out, first thing—'your cat's dead'. You should have broken it to me gently. You could have said: 'Neal, the cat got out the window the other day and crawled up the rainspout and got up on the roof and slipped and fell', and then you could have said it died."

"I'm sorry," apologized Marc.

"Okay, forget it," said Neal. "How's Mom?"

"Well, Mom got out the window the other day and crawled up the rainspout . . ."

The visitor to New York rushed from the airport into a waiting taxi, trying to keep dry in the heavy downpour.

"Can you think of anything worse," grumbled the visitor, "than raining cats and dogs in New York?"

"Sure," said the cab driver, "hailing taxis!"

Henderson knocked on the farmhouse door and a white-haired lady opened it.

"Excuse me," said Henderson, "do you own a calico cat with a red collar and a silver bell attached to it?"

"Yes," said the elderly woman, "that's my cat."

"Well, I just ran over it," explained the man. "I'm terribly sorry. Of course, I'll replace him."

"Then just don't stand there," replied the old lady. "There's a mouse in the kitchen!"

CATACOMB
An implement for grooming cats.

SIGN IN PET SHOP
Attention Cat Lovers! Save Money!
Feed Your cats Lox. Instead of Cream,
They'll drink water!

"The cat is a wonderful animal, just as clean as a whistle."

"Oh, cats aren't so clean."

"Don't argue with me. Cats are very clean. Take a look at the little pussy in the corner. It's always washing its face."

"I don't know about that. Cats don't wash their faces. They wash their feet and wipe them on their faces."

Candolli, a carpet layer, had just finished a big wall-to-wall job. It had taken him all day. Now, as he stepped back to admire his handiwork, Candolli was horrified to notice a small lump right in the middle of the room. In a flash he realized what had happened. His pack of cigarettes was in none of his pockets. Not one to panic, he made sure nobody was watching, then picked up his hammer and pounded on the lump until the carpet was level. Pleased with himself, Candolli went into the kitchen for his tool kit—and there on the table was his pack of cigarettes.

Just then a woman shouted from upstairs: "Elmer, where's the damn cat?"

"Say, Shanahan, are you still seeing pink elephants after you've had a few too many?"

"Something better," replied the Irishman. "Yesterday I dropped some booze in the goldfish bowl, the fish drank it, hopped out of the bowl and chased the cat down the street."

"Your cat was making an awful noise last night."

"You're right. Ever since she ate the canary she thinks she can sing."

Screams of delight piercing the air attested to the fact that Todd's tom cat was indeed the cat's meow. But, after numerous complaints from the neighbors, Todd had a veterinarian render the cat fit to guard a sultan's harem.

Weeks later one of Todd's neighbors said, "I'll bet that ex-tom of yours just lies on the hearth now and gets fat."

"Not exactly," said Todd. "He still goes out. But now he goes along as a consultant."

Did you hear about the all-American cat?

He made fifty yards in one night.

Kerry the cat was scampering all over the neighborhood—down alleys, up fire escapes, down cellars. A lady who knew Kerry's owner knocked on his door. "Your cat is running around like mad."

"I know," said the man. "He's just been neutered, and he's rushing around canceling engagements."

What do you get when you cross a canary with an alley cat?

A peeping tom.

A mouse and a cat walked into a restaurant and sat down. The mouse ordered three kinds of cheese and some grain. The waiter asked what the cat would like, and the mouse answered that the cat wanted nothing.

"Is something the matter?" asked the waiter.

"Hey, if he were hungry," snapped the mouse, "do you think I'd be sitting here?"

ZEBRA
A horse with hashmarks.

"Is it true," the reporter asked the famous explorer, "that wild animals in the jungles won't harm you if you carry a torch?"

"That depends," said the explorer, "on how fast you carry it."

Morgan telephoned his doctor frantically in the middle of the night.

"Come quick. You know my wife always sleeps with her mouth wide open. Well, just now a mouse ran down her throat."

"I'll be over in a few minutes," said the doctor. "Meanwhile, try waving a piece of cheese in front of her mouth and maybe the mouse will come out."

When the M.D. arrived, he found Morgan in his pajamas waving a six-pound flounder frantically in front of his wife's face.

"What's the idea?" said the exasperated doctor, "I told you to wave a piece of cheese. Mice don't like flounders."

"I know," gasped Morgan, "but first we've got to get the cat out."

A rat used for experimental purposes was returned to his cage. He exclaimed to his fellow rats, "You know, I've got Dr. Dubikov conditioned."

"How so?" asked his fellow rats.

"Well, every time I press the bar, he gives me food."

A visitor noticed a stuffed lion in his friend's trophy room and said, "Where did you get this lion?"

"In Africa, when I was on a hunting expedition with my uncle."

"What's the lion stuffed with?"

"My uncle."

Bessie, the cow, sidled over to another Guernsey and said, "Here comes that louse with the icy fingers again."

What's black and white and red all over?
An embarrassed zebra.

Roger Rabbit who came out of his hole one day, and said to his wife, "What a headache I have. Too bad you're so busy having rabbits, or you could go to the drugstore for me!"

Just then a turtle came by. Roger stopped him and said, "Friend turtle, I've got such a headache. Will you go to the drugstore and get me some aspirin?"

The turtle slowly replied, "Sure . . . I . . . will. I'll . . . be . . . right . . . back."

One year and 200 rabbits later, Roger cried, "Why doesn't that turtle hurry with my aspirin."

Finally, four years later, as Roger stood holding his head, off in the distance he saw a turtle coming slowly up the road.

Three days later the turtle arrived and the rabbit said, "Oh, friend turtle, thank heavens you're back. This headache is killing me. Give me the aspirin, quick."

The turtle said, "Mr. ... Rabbit, did ... you say ... Anacin or Bayer's?"

Shaggy Doggerel

Shaggy dog stories are in great demand by humor gourmets. This form of verbal wit requires an unusually sophisticated sense of humor and a shamelessly willing suspension of disbelief. This is a fairly reasonable definition:

> A **shaggy dog** story is a nonsensical joke that employs in the punchline a non sequitur, a punning variation of a familiar saying, or a hoax, to trick the listener who expects conventional wit or humor.

Shaggy dog stories have animals talking and displaying human qualities, people doing absurd deeds and a punchline that very often makes no sense at all. They are silly, ridiculous, full of puns and have absolutely no relationship to reality. But they're great fun.

No one really knows how they got their name but this first joke is considered to be a variation of the original. What follows is a collection of classics:

Gaskell, sitting in a London pub, picked up a year-old copy of the *New York Times* and read an ad offering a large reward for the return of a very shaggy dog to its bereft owner on Long Island.

Ten minutes later Gaskell stumbled over the shaggiest pup ever born. He promptly bundled the canine under his arm, took a freighter from Southampton to New York, and then a taxi all the way out to Montauk Point. Gaskell rushed to the house of the man who advertised and rang his bell.

He opened the door. "Listen," said the Englishman, holding up the pooch, "you lost a shaggy dog, is this it?"

"I should say not," snapped the man, "it wasn't that shaggy!"—and slammed the door in his face.

Two dogs met on the street.

"Bow-wow," said the first.

"Meow," said the second.

"Say, have you gone crazy?"

"No," was the proud reply. "I've been studying foreign languages."

A dog walked into a restaurant and ordered a steak.

"How would you like it cooked?" asked the waiter.

"I like it well done, with crushed cherries on top. Then put some marinated tomatos on it and soak it in Diet Pepsi."

The waiter brought the food.

"Did you enjoy your dinner?" the waiter asked when he was finished.

"Very much," answered the dog. "By the way, don't you think this is all very odd?"

"No," answered the waiter. "I like my steak the same way."

Godwin opened the refrigerator and found his dog sitting inside.

"What are you doing here?" he asked.

"Isn't this a Westinghouse?" asked the dog.

"Yes."

"Well, I'm westing."

Mrs. Cartier-Bresson, a very rich lady, had a dog who had his own little doghouse complete with little furniture. A neighbor was looking at it one day and asked, "How does he keep it so clean?"

"Oh," said the owner, "he has a French poodle come in once a week."

Elton dropped over to visit Dickson, a new Mill Valley neighbor. They were sitting in the den talking when a dog came in and asked if anyone had seen the Sunday *Examiner*. Dickson handed the newspaper to the canine and it left.

"That's remarkable," exclaimed Elton. "A dog that reads."

"Oh, don't let him fool you," said Dickson, "He just looks at the comics."

Two dogs were watching some teenagers gyrate and flail about as they danced to raucous music. After a while one dog turned to the other and said, "When I act like that, they give me worm pills."

One of King Arthur's lesser-known knights was a little man named Sir Kugel. Sir Kugel was a very poor knight; and couldn't even afford a horse. He was forced to ride around on a rented Saint Bernard.

One pitch-black night, Sir Kugel was riding down a path through the woods when a storm started up. The knight turned his St. Bernard around and headed toward a lonely inn a little way off the road.

When he got there he pounded on the door with his spear and asked for shelter.

"Do you have a reservation?" asked the innkeeper.

"No," replied the poor knight.

"Sorry," said the innkeeper, "we're full up." Then he looked down and saw Sir Kugel astride his canine mount. "Oh, well," he reconsidered, "come on in. We'll make room for you somehow. I wouldn't turn out a knight on a dog like this."

What happened when the riverboat captain peeled onions?

It made the Bridge on the River Kwai.

A gorilla walked into Kaplan's New York delicatessen and ordered a pastrami sandwich on pumpernickel with a piece of pickle on the side to go.

"That'll be eight dollars," said Kaplan, handing the ape the sandwich. "And I gotta say, I never expected to see a gorilla in my store!"

"At eight dollars for a pastrami sandwich," snapped the gorilla, "you never will again!"

Two caterpillars, Enoch and Silas, were sunning themselves in the garden. A small shadow fell across them and they glanced up to see a butterfly overhead. It fluttered, swooped and did a few fancy acrobatic turns on the air currents.

"Listen," said Silas, "there's one thing for sure, you'll never get me up in one of those contraptions."

A leopard who visited his optometrist complained, "Every time I look at my wife, I see spots before my eyes."

"What do you expect?" scoffed the optometrist. "You're a leopard, aren't you?"

"Sure," conceded the leopard, "but my wife is a zebra."

Perkins seated in a movie theatre noticed that the man in front of him had his arm around the neck of a huge Afghan hound which occupied the seat next to him.

The dog was watching the picture with obvious understanding, for he snarled softly when the villain spoke, and yelped joyously at the funny lines.

Perkins leaned over and tapped the man in front of him on the shoulder. "Excuse me, but I can't get over your dog's behavior."

"Yeah, I'm surprised, too," said the man. "He hated the book."

While strolling through Central Park, Silsby spotted a grasshopper hopping around. "Hello, friend grasshopper," said Silsby, "did you know they've named a drink after you?"

"Really?" replied the grasshopper, "they've named a drink Bartholemew?"

Three men and a dog were sitting around a table playing poker. As the evening wore on, the woman of the household came in and almost fainted at seeing the dog playing cards.

"That's the most amazing thing I've ever seen, a dog playing poker!" she sputtered.

"What's so amazing?" barked the dog. "I haven't won a hand yet."

Dobson was taking his horse into a subway when a guard rushed up to him yelling, "Hey, where are you going? Don't you know it's against the law to take a horse on the subway?"

"Yeah, I know," said Dobson, "but he always gets sick on the bus."

The science reporter had been waiting for his entire career to be able to write the headline and finally NASA obliged. They sent a bunch of cows into space aboard the payload bay of the shuttle. The next day the newspaper told all about "The Herd Shot Round the World."

Blackwell, the famous dog trainer, gave a party in honor of his talented Alsatian. As part of the entertainment, the hound lumbered over to the baby grand, climbed on the stool and proceeded to play a Bach sonata. Halfway through, one of the guests spoke too loudly and the animal growled and chased the heckler into a corner.

"Don't worry," said Blackwell, "his Bach is worse than his bite."

A beagle was complaining to a basset that he felt poorly. "Nothing physical," he said. "Just bored, always tired, never really in top form."

"Well," said the basset, "why don't you see a psychiatrist?"

"How can I see a psychiatrist?" said the beagle. "You know I'm not allowed on couches."

Chadwick the ventriloquist was on the way down to a bar for a drink when a big shaggy dog fell in at his side.

They went in, the ventriloquist ordered a scotch and for a laugh he looked down at the dog and said, "Well, are you having the usual?"

"No, thanks, I've had enough this morning," said the dog.

The barman was flabbergasted. He offered $50 for the animal.

"No, sir!" said Chadwick, "I've had him since he was a pup."

"I'll make it a hundred bucks!" said the bartender.

Chadwick shook his head. When the offer went to $500 the ventriloquist grabbed the money and headed for the door. "All right," he added, "take good care of him." With a last look at the dog, "Farewell, old pal!"

"Old pal, my foot!" said the dog, "after what you've just done I'll never speak to another human as long as I live."

Morrissey and his dog were sitting at a bar. He ordered two martinis. Benson handed one to the dog who promptly drank it, then ate the glass until only the base and stem remained. Then he left.

"That's the craziest thing I've ever seen," said the bartender.

"Yeah, he's a dumb dog," said Morrissey. "The stem is the best part."

Dixon walked into the saloon and asked for a double bourbon.

Suddenly he looked up and realized that tending bar, apron and all, was a large dog.

"What's the matter," asked the canine. "Haven't you ever seen a dog tending bar before?"

"Oh, it's not that," said Dixon. "What happened to the horse? Did he sell the joint to you?"

Two collies trotted down the avenue for their morning walk and found that parking meters had been installed on the sidewalk.

"How do you like that?" remarked one pooch to the other. "Pay toilets!"

Three storks were having dinner. The father stork said, "Today, I left a little boy at the Benson's and they were so happy!"

And the mother stork said, "I left twins at the Winslow's and they were so thrilled!"

Just then the father stork said, "And son, what did you do today?"

"Nothing much," said the baby stork. "I just scared the hell out of some college kids!"

Mama Skunk was worried because she never could keep track of her two children. They were named In and Out, and whenever In was in, Out was out, and if Out was in, In was out. One day she called Out in and hold him to go out and bring In in. So Out went out and in no time at all he brought In in.

"Wonderful!" said Mama Skunk. "How, in all this great forest, could you find In in so short a time?"

"It was easy," said Out. "In stinct."

Thompkins tapped on the sleeping parakeet's cage and said, "Hey, birdie, can you talk?"

"Sure," said the bird, "can you fly?"

Two microbes were living in the lymph stream of a horse. One day they decided to move over to his blood stream. Thirty minutes after they did, some penicillin came along and killed them.

The moral: Don't change streams in the middle of a horse.

Mogumba the African king had an obsession for thrones. He collected hundreds of them. Mogumba squeezed and crowded the thrones into his grass hut until it was piled so high the hut collapsed and crushed the king to death.

The moral: People who live in grass houses shouldn't stow thrones.

Kellem killed his vicious horse and had to dispose of the corpse. He was able to sell the flesh and the skin but was left with all the bones. He took them in a boat to dump them in the middle of a lake but a storm came up, overturned the boat and Kellem drowned.

The moral: People who live with cross horses shouldn't row bones.

During the days of ancient Greece, Benny, a handsome boy, was granted eternal youth by Zeus on the condition that he didn't shave. If he shaved, he would turn into ashes and be placed in an urn.

Benny lived for centuries without shaving until the 20th century when he finally shaved and the curse was carried out.

The moral: A Benny shaved is a Benny urned.

A lion finished eating a bull and began to roar. A hunter heard the noise and killed the mighty lion.

The moral: When you're full of bull, keep your mouth shut.

A journalist was sent to find photographer Tanaki Rhee, who had been lost in New Guinea while on assignment for *Life* magazine. After months of searching through the steaming jungles, he finally came upon a small village where several outsiders were held in deep, murky pits.

Shining a flashlight into one pit after another, the journalist at last spotted his quarry. Jumping for joy, he sang out, "Oh, sweet Mr. Rhee of *Life*, at last I've found you!"

A Newark bookie was given a parrot in lieu of cash payment. The bird's vocabulary included choice phrases of German, French, Russian, and English. Sensing a winner, the bookie brought the bird to his favorite bar.

"Wanna bet his bird can speak four languages?" the bookie said to the bartender.

The bartender agreed to a $50 wager. The bookie turned to the parrot and said, "Parlez-vous francais?"

There was no response.

Nor was there any reply to the question in English, Russian or German. The bartender picked up the bookie's money from the bar and went about his business.

On the street, the bookie glared at the bird. "You fink!" he exclaimed. "I got $50 riding on you and you clam up on me. I oughta strangle you."

"Don't be a jerk," replied the parrot. "Just think of the odds you'll get tomorrow."

An elephant crashing through the jungle, noticed a movement near one of his fore-hooves. He stopped and peered down. A tiny mouse peeped up at him. The elephant said, "You're the puniest, most insignificant object I've ever laid eyes on."

Squeaked the mouse, "But I've been sick!"

Two sharks were frolicking in the Atlantic near the New York shoreline. "Take my tip and stay clear of Coney Island," said one shark to the other. "Herman was swimming down there last weekend and he got mugged."

One July morning, farmer Nelson started to town with horse and wagon. Halfway in, the horse stopped, turned his head and said, "Sakes alive, but it's hot."

The amazed farmer turned to his dog riding beside him asked, "Did you hear what I heard?"

"Yeah," said the dog, "but he's like everyone else—always talking about the weather and never doing anything about it."

Ellis offered to sell a German shepherd to Bostwick for $20, claiming it was a talking dog. "Please buy me," said the canine. "My owner is mean to me, and he beats me with a whip. And I'm really a good dog. I've won seven blue ribbons at the biggest and best kennel clubs."

"That German shepherd really does talk," gasped Bostwick. "Why do you want to sell him for only $20?"

"Because," said the dog's owner, "I can't stand a liar."

One dachshund met another when he turned around to scratch. "You are very beautiful. I think I would like to marry you," he declared.

"Don't be a dope," was the reply. "I'm your other end."

Farmer Selkirk's collie had just died. He was bemoaning his loss when a little cocker spaniel walked up to him and said, "I heard your collie is dead. How about giving me a job?"

"You!" gasped Selkirk. "How could a little fellow like you take the place of my big dog?"

"I'll show you."

He leaped into the driver's seat of the tractor, operated the machine perfectly, turned off the ignition, trotted over to the stable and milked three cows.

"How's that?" he asked the farmer.

"Very good," said Selkirk, "but let me see how you shuck corn."

"Hold it!" exclaimed the cocker spaniel. "Who ever heard of a cocker that could shuck corn!"

A newly crowned African chief was so religious that he forebade the killing of animals.

Not long thereafter, the lion and tiger population got so large they began feeding on humans. Soon, even the antelope and zebra were so plentiful that they began nibbling on natives. The terrified populace petitioned their leader to rescind his edict, but he refused. They had no choice but to overthrow the chief. Not only was the revolt successful, it was the first time in history that a reign was called on account of game.

Two herrings, Cain and Abel, went to a bar regularly for refreshment. One day Cain showed up alone and the bartender asked, "Where's your brother?"

"How should I know," said Cain. "Am I my brother's kipper?"

A little girl born to an Italian mother and a Jewish father was named Carmen Cohen. Her mother used only her first name and father the last name. The poor girl grew up never knowing whether she was Carmen or Cohen.

Wingate, an elderly widower, went to a country auction. A parrot was put up for bidding and he decided that the bird might be good company for him on lonely evenings. The bidding grew stiff.

$50 ... $75 ... $100. Wingate got carried away by the spirit of the occasion and before he realized it, he bought the parrot for $200.

The widower carried the bird home and stood it on the table before him. "Now," he commanded, "talk to me!"

The parrot drew in its head and glared at him.

"I said talk to me," repeated Wingate. "After all, I bought you to keep me company."

Again the parrot said nothing.

"Good heavens," he cried. "You mean to say that after what I paid for you, you can't even talk?"

"Can't even talk?" echoed the parrot. "Who in hell do you think it was that bid you up to $200."

A dog won a blue ribbon in a show and then left it behind in a bar. His son was sent back to the saloon to get it. "What'll you have?" asked the bartender.

"Pap's blue ribbon."

Objects made of teak were stolen from a man named Chan by a bear with feet like a boy. After a month-long chase they finally caught the "boy-foot bear with teak of Chan."

Burton and his wife were driving through the country one lovely Sunday afternoon when suddenly a dog pulled up alongside, forced them to the side of the road, and whipped out a notebook.

"Whatever is that dog doing?" asked Mrs. Burton.

"Writing out a ticket, silly," replied her husband. "Can't you see he's a police dog?"

Donavan ordered a scotch in a Denver bar. When it came he withdrew a mouse from his coat pocket, and after he belted the drink down, allowed the creature to finish the few drops that remained. Suddenly the mouse burst into an aria from *La Traviata*, singing in a brilliant tenor.

A customer standing nearby couldn't believe his eyes. "How much you want for the mouse?"

"Heck," said Donavan. "Buy me a bottle of scotch and you can have him."

The deal was made and the new owner departed. "You must be crazy," said the bartender. "Why did you give away a fortune like that for one lousy bottle of scotch?"

"Eh-h," said Donavan, "that mouse can sing only in Italian."

A family of bears were rummaging in a Wyoming national park garbage dump. Suddenly, a car crammed with eight tourists pulled up at the side of the road. "It's cruel," cried the Papa Bear to his brood, "to keep them caged up like that!"

"Tell me about your work. What do you do?"

"Well, I'm a stunt man. I wrestle alligators underwater, and lions and tigers on land. I leap off cliffs and jump from tall buildings."

"My goodness! How do you manage to stay alive?"

"I take in laundry on the side."

"I've got an act I think you could use," Retting said to the TV producer.

Out of one pocket he took a mouse and a miniature piano, which he placed on the producer's desk. Out of the other Retting took a beautiful butterfly. At once the mouse began to play and the butterfly began to sing an aria from the opera *Carmen*.

"That is absolutely sensational!" cried the producer. "Name your price."

"Well," said Retting, "there is one thing you should know. The act really isn't as good as it seems. You see, the butterfly can't really sing. The mouse is a ventriloquist."

Farnsworth walked into a Portland bar and said to the bartender, "Give me a beer and a shot of whiskey."

Farnsworth drank the beer, poured the liquor into his pocket and ordered another round. Once again, he guzzled down the beer and poured the whiskey into his pocket.

Farnsworth did the same thing again and finally the bartender could stand it no longer. "Hey, buddy," he shouted, "how come you keep pouring the booze into your pocket?"

"It's none of your damn business!" screamed Farnsworth, "and if you give me a hard time, I'll punch you in the mouth!"

Just then, a mouse popped out of his pocket and exclaimed, "And that goes for your damn cat too!"

The king of an African tribe had a high fever. To cure him, the witch doctor cut a leather thong into twelve pieces and told him to eat one part each day. It didn't work. The king said, "The thong is gone, but the malady lingers on."

The Okefenokee swamp in Georgia was the scene of the recent International Insects Convention. A bunch of mosquitoes on a tree stump were reminiscing.

"I wish I lived in the good old days before DDT," said Horace. "That stuff sure makes it rough on us."

Several other young mosquitoes agreed, when an old timer interrupted. "Sure, it's a little rough in some ways these days," he agreed, "but it's so much better in others."

"Like what?" asked Horace.

"Well, son," answered the old one, "when I was your age, we could bite a girl only on the arms or the face, but look at the opportunities you fellas have today!"

The caravan made its way slowly over the burning desert. Two camels trudged along side by side. Finally, one of them looked around furtively and spoke.

"I don't care what anybody says," he whispered, "I'm thirsty."

Anderson entered a Philadelphia tavern and found the bartender playing chess with a dog. The dog, watching the board intently, made his moves by grasping the particular chessmen in his teeth. He wagged his tail wildly when he made a good move and, on occasion, would bark sharply to indicate "Check!"

Anderson, recovering from his amazement, gasped, "Hey, that's some smart dog you've got there."

"Not so smart!" said the barkeep. "I beat him three times out of five so far."

Ivan, a Russian Communist, was visiting close friends Rudolph and his wife Ninotchka. After a glass of tea, Rudolph said, "It will rain tonight."

"I don't believe it," said Ivan.

"Please," said Ninotchka, "Rudolph the Red knows rain, dear."

Mrs. Bryce thought that $20 was a very reasonable price for a thoroughbred police dog. She clipped out the ad from the Kansas newspaper that proclaimed this extraordinary bargain, wrote out a check, and ordered the dog to be shipped to her residence.

A few days later the delivery man deposited on her doorstep the mangiest-looking mongrel she had ever seen. In a rage, Mrs. Bryce telephoned the man who had inserted the ad, and said, "What do you mean by calling that mutt a thoroughbred police dog?"

"Don't be deceived by his looks," was the reply. "He's in the Secret Service."

In Colorado an elderly Indian named Shortcake died. The town's undertaker called on the widow to make the funeral arrangements. His wife said, "Too late. Squaw bury Shortcake."

A man's hat came floating down the river. As it passed, the fisherman on the bank was amazed to see it rise and reveal a face underneath.

"Am I heading for New Orleans?" asked a voice.

"Straight ahead," said the fisherman.

"Thanks," said the voice and the hat went floating down the river once more.

The fisherman shouted after it, "You've got a long, long way to go."

The hat rose once more and the voice said, "That's all right, I'm on my brother's bike."

Armstrong's ear was bleeding profusely. "I bit myself," he explained to the doctor.

"That's impossible," said the M.D. "How can a man possibly bite himself on the ear?"

"I was standing on a chair."

Fuller sat down at a soda fountain and said to the clerk, "Gimme a soda, without flavor."

"Without flavor?" asked the clerk.

"Without vanilla."

"Ain't got no vanilla."

"All right, gimme one without strawberry."

Gilmer was born with a golden screw in his navel. When he grew up, the golden screw became so annoying he decided to have it removed. He went to the Mayo Clinic, and was told that the golden screw could not be removed. The surgeon suggested a seer in Bombay.

Gilmer went to India. The seer said that the screw could not and should not be removed. Gilmer insisted, so the seer sent him to a holy man in Egypt.

The holy man said, "During the next full moon, go to the Great Sphinx, lie on your back naked, and repeat three times, 'Allah, please remove the golden screw from my navel.' "

The night of the full moon, Gilmer went to the Great Sphinx, removed his clothing, lay on his back, and three times asked for Allah's help.

Suddenly there appeared a bright, shining dot. It came closer and closer. The object was a gold screwdriver. It hovered above him. Then slowly the screwdriver began to unscrew the golden screw. The screw was removed!

At last Gilmer was rid of the golden screw! He leaped up and his butt fell off!

Geoffrey and Bryant were swapping funny stories at a bar when a huge St. Bernard entered, took a stool next to them, and ordered a drink.

"Careful now, Bryant," said Geoffrey. "No more shaggy dog stories."

Business Boffs

One afternoon an advertising vice-president called the whole staff in to hear a couple of jokes he'd picked up at lunch.

Everybody laughed uproariously except Joyce, who sat there with a glum expression on her face.

The man next to her nudged her and whispered. "What's the matter? Haven't you got a sense of humor?"

"I don't have to laugh," replied Joyce. "I'm quitting Friday."

Did you hear about the corporate wife who claims that if you give a man enough rope, he'll claim he's tied up at the office?

The senile chairman of the board walked into the meeting, ponderously took his seat, and looked to his left.

"My word," he muttered, "look at you, Keegan! You've lost weight, got rid of your eyeglasses, and—correct me if I'm wrong—but even the color of your hair is different."

The senior VP squirmed uneasily. "Excuse me, Mr. Eisner, but . . . I'm not Keegan."

"Good Lord!" exclaimed the old man, "you've even changed your name!"

Griffin and Hickman were discussing a mutual acquaintance. "He used to work for me," said Griffin. "I wouldn't trust him with my money. He'd lie, steal, cheat—anything for a buck."

"How do you know him so well?" asked Hickman.

"How? I taught him everything he knows!"

At a testimonial dinner Werbell, the guest of honor, said, "When I came to this country I had only one suit on my back, one pair of shoes on my feet and everything I owned was wrapped in a red handkerchief I carried on my shoulder. Now I own buildings, banks, cars, houses. Which proves this is a great country. Anybody who works hard can make it."

One young man said, "What did you have in the red handkerchief?"

Werbell said, "About $500,000 in cash, a million in diamonds and a few negotiable securities."

The senior VP shuffled into his house and was greeted by his wife.

"Ralph," she said, startled, "what are you doing home so early?"

"The boss and I had a fight," he grumbled. "He wouldn't take back what he said."

Beaming with pride, the woman asked, "What did he say?"

The senior VP shrugged. "You're fired."

"Always remember," said Switzer to his son, "there are two things that will ensure your success in business."

"What are they?"

"Integrity and wisdom," said Switzer.

"Integrity?"

"That's right. No matter how it may be to your detriment, no matter what your colleagues or the board may say, always keep your word once you have given it."

"And wisdom?"

"Don't be a horse's ass and give it."

A secretary was complaining to another girl in the office. "I'm sick of marriage. Kenneth hasn't kissed me once since I came back from my honeymoon."

The other girl said, "Then why don't you divorce him?" The first girl said, "I'm not married to Kenneth."

"Miss Lopez, I was just reading over this letter you did. Your typing is really improving. I see there are only seven mistakes here."

"Thank you, sir."

"Now, let's take a look at the second line."

Have you heard the one about the executive who was so old that when he chased his secretary around the desk, he couldn't remember why?

Boss:	Are you doing anything on Sunday evening?
Beautiful secretary (hopefully):	No.
Boss:	Then it shouldn't be hard for you to get in on time Monday morning.

Vicky returned from a coffee break and found her boss gazing dumbfounded into the file drawer labeled T-Z.

"Vicky," exclaimed the puzzled man, "where on earth do

you keep the Zachary correspondence? This file drawer is completely empty."

"Zachary?" asked the secretary. "Let's see now, is that a company or an individual?"

"What possible difference does that make?" demanded her employer.

"Well, I should say it makes a lot of difference," bristled the girl. "I don't know whether it would be filed under D for Dear Sir or under G for Gentlemen."

The new secretary ended her first day on the job by inquiring of the bookkeeper, "Doesn't that sourpuss boss of yours ever laugh out loud?"

"Only," sighed the bookkeeper, "if we ask him for a raise."

Employer: (to newly hired secretary) Now, I hope you understand the importance of punctuation.
Secretary: Oh, yes indeed, sir. I always get to work on time.

Quirox was applying for a job. "Now this is the verbal part of your employment test," said the personnel manager. "What does Aurora Borealis mean?"

"It means I don't get this job!"

Fink and Geller were partners. While they were having lunch, Fink shouted, "Oh, my God!"

"Whatsa matta?" asked Geller.

"We went away," said Fink, "and we left the safe open!"

"Whatta you worried about?" said his partner. "We're both here!"

Potter picked up his first tailored suit and was disgusted with the results. The seams were uneven, there was too much fabric on the back, and the collar was considerably higher on the back than on the sides. But he was late for a meeting, and, having no choice, Potter wore the suit.

As he stood waiting for a cab, an immaculately dressed stranger walked over. "Pardon me," he asked, "but who's your tailor?"

"Why on earth do you want to know?" said Potter.

"Because," he replied, "anyone who can fit a hunchback so well is certainly going to get my business."

An Austin real estate developer phoned a friend and said, "J.J., ah'm in big trouble. Ah'm about ta go bankrupt—unless ah kin raise some cash—and ah haven't the slightest idea where ah'm gonna git it from."

"Ah'm glad to hear it," said his friend. "For a minute there ah was afraid yew might think yew could borrow it from me!"

Customer: What do you mean! Eight hundred dollars for that antique! Last week you wanted only $500.
Burgess: Well, you know how the cost of labor and materials keeps going up.

Vandakis sold hot dogs from a cart on 56th Street. "How's business?" asked an acquaintance.

"Could be worse!" said Vandakis. "I put away already $2000 in the bank!"

"That's good," said the friend. "Maybe you could lend me $50?"

"I ain't allowed!"

"Whaddaya mean not *allowed*?"

"I make an agreement with the bank. They agreed not to sell hot dogs if I promised I wouldn't make loans!"

This past season in New York, business was so bad the dress manufacturers were firing their sons-in-law.

Dunnagan heard that a company he was billing was about to fail. He rushed over and said to the owner, "Is it true that you're going into bankruptcy?"

"Yes, but I'm making you a preferred creditor."

"What's a preferred creditor?"

"Well, I'm telling you now that you're not going to get anything. The others won't know it for sixty to ninety days yet."

SIGN IN FRONT OF BANKRUPT STORE
We undersold everybody.

Margolis and Platt met at Palm Beach. "How are things with you?" asked Margolis.

"The dress business is so bad," complained Platt. "This last year I've been losing $500 a week. And that's week after week after week!"

"So why don't you give up the business?"

"So how am I gonna make a living?"

Ira: (Telephoning his partner from Miami) How's everything in New York?
Lou: Everything's all right.
Ira: How's the weather?
Lou: How should the weather be?
Ira: How's business in the shop?
Lou: It's fine, but I got bad news for you.
Ira: Whatsa matta?
Lou: We've been robbed!
Ira: Don't be silly, Lou! Put it back!

"I can't understand it," said Straus to his partner Ponsford. "Here we are bankrupt, through, finished—and only yesterday the President said that business was booming!"

"Maybe," said Ponsford, "the President has a better location!"

CLOTHING MANUFACTURER'S MAXIM
The nicest thing about money
is that it never clashes with
anything you're wearing.

Butterfield rented space at one of those outdoor California swap meets. A woman customer picked up a broken fork and asked, "How much?"

"A penny," said Butterfield.

"A penny!" grumbled the woman. "That's too much!"

"Make me an offer."

O'Connell got a job driving a bus. At the end of the first day he turned in the receipts—$112. The next day's returns were $168. On the third day, he brought in $98. But, on the fourth day, he gave the cashier $312.

"This is great!" exclaimed the cashier. "That route never brought in that much money. What happened?"

"After three days on that lousy route," explained O'Connell, "I figured business wasn't gonna get any better, so I drove over to Broadway and worked there. Say, that street is a regular gold mine!"

Miller and Glick met on Seventh Avenue. "How's business?" asked Miller.

"Lousy!" answered Glick. "On Monday, I sold only one suit all day. Tuesday, business was so bad the salesmen were trying to sell each other. And Wednesday, was worse, yet. The man that bought the suit Monday brought it back!"

Fur coat manufacturers Lubin and Raskin were basking in the Puerto Rican sunshine. "You took your son, the college boy, into the business. How's he working out?" asked Lubin.

"You wouldn't believe it!" replied Raskin. "He wants to cross mink with kangaroo to get fur coats with pockets in them!"

Traverso owed $1000 to Matson. The debt was past due and Traverso was broke so he borrowed the $1000 from Halsted and paid Matson.

A week later, Traverso borrowed back the $1000 from Matson and paid Halsted. Another week went by and Traverso borrowed back the $1000 from Halsted to pay Matson.

He repeated this transaction several times, until finally he called them up and said, "Fellas, this is a lotta bother. Why don't you two exchange the $1000 every week and keep me out of it!"

"Is your son a good executive?" asked Spivak.

"My boy is so dedicated to his work," said Weber, "that he keeps his secretary near his bed in case he gets an idea during the night!"

This Texas newspaper ad for automobiles is a timely reflection of business conditions in the Lone Star state:

"Buy a new car today and get your choice of a free tape deck or an office building in downtown Houston.

"Act now! The tape decks are going fast!"

As in most businesses, nepotism is very much part of the motion picture industry. At one time, the head of a large studio brought in the boy who had married his daughter and made him production chief.

Within six months, the young man produced three pictures that were financial disasters. The father-in-law called the boy into his office.

"It's not bad enough," he screamed, "that the movies you made were lousy. And that you lost millions of dollars. But you set the son-in-law business back twenty years!"

"Meyer, you took your son-in-law into the dress business with you, how's he doin'?"

"It's amazing," said Meyer. "He's been with me now only two weeks and already he's a month behind on his work!"

During the French Revolution, when the guillotine was being used almost around the clock, Toussaint lived in a small village outside of Paris. One morning he met Dumas, who had just returned from the city.

"What's happening there in Paris?" asked Toussaint.

"Conditions are absolutely horrible," replied the Frenchman. "They're cutting off heads by the thousands."

"Mon Dieu!" moaned Toussaint, "and me in the hat business!"

Customer: Is this suit all wool?
Rothstein: I won't lie to you. It's not. The buttons are covered in silk.

Adler and Krantz, ladies lingerie manufacturers, were sitting in a restaurant during the slack season.

"Did you hear about Barney?" asked Adler. "His place burned down."

"Yeah?" said Krantz. "He's a nice fellow. He deserves it."

One bright school morning the teacher turned to her class and asked, "All those pupils who want to go to heaven, raise your hands."

All hands except little Melvin's went up.

The teacher asked him, "Don't you want to go to heaven?"

"I heard my father tell my mother that 'Business has gone to hell,' " replied Melvin, "and I want to go where the business is."

Two cloak and suit manufacturers, Billig and Plimpkin, were sitting in their empty office wailing over the sudden drop in business. "I wish Gabriel would blow his horn," said Billig.

"Why?" asked Plimpkin.

"All the dead people'll come to life," explained Billig, "and they'll all need clothes."

MEDICAL NEWS UPDATE
Surgeons successfully transplanted a shark's heart
into a businessman's body. The patient has fully
recovered and is now a Senior Partner in
a major Chicago law firm.

"I can't understand why you failed in business."

"Too much advertising."

"You never spent a cent in your life on advertising."

"That's true, but my competitor did."

Felder owned a store that had recently been burglarized. He met Baker, a friend, on the street.

"I'm sorry to hear about the robbery," said Baker. "Did you lose much?"

"Some," replied the storekeeper. "But it woulda been a lot worse if the burglar broke in the night before."

"Why?" asked the friend.

"Well," said Felder, "just the day of the robbery I marked everything down twenty percent."

Harvey's boss was a tyrant and Harvey was very timid. Harvey went to him and said, "I'd like one week off."

"Why?" demanded the boss.

"I'm getting married tomorrow, sir. And it would give me great pleasure to accompany my young wife on her honeymoon."

Cecelia applied for a job in a big company. The office manager asked her if she had any unusual talents. "I won quite a few contests in crossword puzzles and slogan writing," she replied.

"Sounds good," said the manager, "but we want somebody who will be smart during office hours."

"Oh, this *was* during office hours."

WINDOW SIGN IN COLUMBUS CLOTHING STORE
Use our easy credit plan: 100% down—
nothing to pay each month!

Korwin and Roth, two garment manufacturers, met on Seventh Avenue.

"Good morning!" offered Korwin.

"Don't talk to me," replied Roth. "You're so crooked that the wool you've been pulling over my eyes is 50 per cent polyester."

Customer: If that coat cost you $100, how can you afford to sell it to me for $60?
Owner: Sh-h-h, my friend. I sell a lot of coats. That's how I can do it!

Pluth, a delivery man from Hartford making his first trip to New York, saw the sign CLIMB ONE FLIGHT AND SAVE FIFTY DOLLARS ON A NEW SUIT. He climbed and immediately was shown a number of shoddy garments by Rapp, the eager salesman. Pluth refused to bite.

Rapp knew that Rudnick, the boss, was watching him, so he made a special effort with his next number. Rapp whirled the customer around and around before the mirror, crying, "It fits like a glove! You look like a movie star!"

When Pluth again said "No," Rudnick took over, produced one blue gabardine suit, and made the sale in five minutes. As Pluth left, the boss said, "You see how easy it is when you know how. He went for the first suit I showed him."

"Yeah," agreed Rapp, "but who made him dizzy?"

Swegel, to stay in business, always insisted on having his checks dated ahead, so they let him do it. But even with that advantage, he died and his tombstone reads:

"Here lies the body of Lynwood Swegel—died June 15, as of July 1."

SIGN IN PITTSBURGH CLOTHING STORE
These pants will look better on your legs
than on our hands.

Tafel worked for a Rhode Island company for twenty-five years, then was let go. He asked for a letter of recommendation and the employer wrote this for him:

"TO WHOM IT MAY CONCERN: Mr. R. Tafel worked for us for twenty-five years and when he left we were perfectly satisfied."

Swisher, a manufacturer of leather goods in Illinois, received word from another rep that his top traveling salesman died of a heart attack in a Houston hotel.

Swisher sent this telegram—collect:

"Return samples by freight and search his pants for orders."

Dr. Campbell the optician was instructing his new assistant. "Now, son, we want to get a fair and honest price out of every customer. After you have fitted the glasses and the customer asks 'What's the charge?' you say, 'The charge is fifty dollars.'

"Then you pause. If the customer doesn't flinch, you say, 'That's for the frames; the lenses will be another fifty dollars.' Then you pause, and again you wait. And if the customer doesn't flinch, you say 'Each.' "

A schoolteacher bought a used car. The next day she drove it back to the dealer's lot. "What's wrong?" he asked.

"Nothing," said the teacher. "I just want to return these things for the dear old lady you told me owned the car before you sold it to me. She left this box of cigars in the glove compartment and this half-empty bottle of scotch under the seat."

1st Partner: I don't like the new bookkeeper you hired. She limps and she stutters.
2nd Partner: What of it?
1st Partner: Why did you hire her?
2nd Partner: So she'll be easy to identify if she steals.

Mowrey, the biggest mortician in town, was complaining to a friend who had come to visit him at the funeral parlor. "Business sure is off."

"How bad can things be?" retorted the friend. "All four of these caskets are occupied."

Just then two bodies sat up and Mowrey's friend turned ashen.

"Don't get upset," said Mowrey, "they're just my partners trying to make the place look busy."

Two bank robbers hit a small bank in the Nashville suburbs one morning and herded everyone into the vault at gunpoint. They gagged Grugan, the bank manager, bound him hand and foot and forced him to the floor of the cashiers cage.

Suddenly, Grugan began to gesture with his head that he wanted to say something. After stuffing the money into sacks, they removed Grugan's gag.

"Give me a break, fellas," he pleaded. "Take the books with you. I'm thirty-two thousand dollars short."

Vale and Shaw, two successful small town shopkeepers, were arguing over business ethics.

"I'll tell you one thing," said Vale, "there are lots of ways to make money, but there is only one honest way."

"What way is that?" asked Shaw.

"Just what I thought," said Vale. "You don't know."

Customer: How much are your $50 shoes?
Salesman: Twenty-five dollars a foot.

Bigelow was teaching his new son-in-law the jewelry business. "This is my best money maker," he said, pointing to a case of wristwatches. "They cost me seventy dollars and I sell them for seventy dollars."

"If they cost you seventy bucks and you sell them for seventy bucks, where does your profit come in?" asked the boy.

"That comes from repairing them."

MacAlpin took his son to the state fair. The youngster got on the parachute ride and was caught by the dangling ropes. When he was being pulled heavenward the crowd stood aghast as he hung head downward. Suddenly, MacAlpin shouted, "Angus! Angus! Throw out some of our business cards!"

In a small village in Russia, a marriage broker was trying to arrange a match between Natasha, a beautiful young girl, and Zhukov, a businessman. But Zhukov was stubborn. "Before I buy goods from a mill," he said, "I look at swatches. Before I get married, I gotta have a sample also."

"But my God!" exclaimed the marriage broker, "you can't ask a decent, respectable girl for a thing like that!"

"I am a businessman," said Zhukov, "and that's the way it's gonna be done!"

The broker went off sadly to talk to Natasha. "I've got a fine fella for you," he began. "Lotsa money. A-1 rating. But he's a little eccentric. He says he's a good businessman and he won't go into anything blind. He insists on a sample."

"Listen," said the girl, "I'm as good a businessman as he is. Samples I wouldn't give him. But I will give him references!"

Timeless Tailwaggers

Stanton went down to the airport to pick up his friend Dillon. When he got there Dillon was terribly upset. He said, "I lost the best part of my baggage on the way here."

"Did you misplace it on the plane or was it stolen?" asked Stanton.

"No," said Dillon, "the cork came out!"

"Is your wife a good cook?"

"Let's just say that when my wife takes the TV dinner out of the oven and removes the aluminum foil, she's throwing away the best part."

Did you hear from the guy who just bought a raffle ticket from a charity group?

They were selling chances on a 1995 parking space.

Joe: I sure do miss my mom's apple pie baking.
Bob: I don't. My mother made a fruit cake. I think the ingredients are fruit, nuts and cement. Thanks to her cake I am now suffering from a new stomach ailment. Crushed ulcers.

The circus strong man dipped a sponge in water and squeezed until every drop of water was out of it. Then he invited anyone who wished to come up on stage and try to squeeze another drop out of the sponge. He offered a hundred dollars as a prize.

Ten men tried and failed. Fullmer, age 73, came up and squeezed at least ten more drops out of the sponge.

"That's incredible," said the strong man. "How could you do that?"

"Easy," said Fullmer. "For 20 years I've been collecting for the United Fund."

Did you hear about the college boy who sent his father a hundred dollar check for Christmas?

His father signed it and sent it back.

A college kid wrote home: "Dear Pop. I'm worried about you, haven't heard from you in weeks. Please send me a check immediately so I'll know you're okay."

Cindy, an Arizona State University freshman, wired her mother that she needed fifty dollars. "I've had five dates with Dirk and have worn each of the dresses I brought with me. I have a date with him on Saturday night and must have another dress immediately."

Her mother wired back: "Get another boyfriend and start all over."

Sending a kid through college could be very educational. It teaches parents to do without a lot of things.

Why did God make man before He made woman?

Because He didn't want any advice on how to do it.

Shockley was mountain climbing. He stumbled and fell over a cliff that was a thousand feet from the ground. He grabbed on to the branch of a tree and hung on for dear life. Shockley looked up to heaven and shouted, "Is there anyone up there?"

No answer.

Again he cried, "Is there anyone up there?"

And out of the clouds came a voice, "Yes, my son. Let go of the branch and I will bear thee up."

Shockley said, "Eh . . . is there anyone else?"

Skeeter and Mickey, two vagrants, were brought before a judge for vagrancy. "Where do you live?" asked the judge.

Skeeter said, "My home is everywhere, the fields, the woods, the beach, the parks . . ."

"What about you?" said the judge to Mickey, "where do you live?"

He said, "I live next door to him!"

A hillbilly couple just got married and the gal said, "Jethro, when did yew first realize that yew loved me?"

He said, "When ah first started gettin' mad at people who tole me yew was dirty, dumb and ugly."

Effie Sue and Burl were having a bad fight. "We're only married five months," said Effie Sue, "and already yew got yoreself a girlfriend."

"Ah, honey," said Burl, "ah ain't got me no other gal. Yew're the only one."

"Don't lie to me! This week alone yew washed yore feet three times already."

Did you hear about the drunk staggering up to the parking meter, inserting a quarter and shouting, "My God! I weigh an hour!"

The hillbilly couple were screeching at each other. The woman shouted, "Aw, yew're so dumb yew think Barnum and Bailey are married to each other!"

The husband said, "What difference does it make, as long as they love each other."

Who are the six most important people at a hillbilly wedding?

The preacher, the bride, the groom and their three kids.

A Kentucky hillbilly woman telephoned the capitol building in Frankfort and asked to speak to the Game Warden. After she was switched to a couple of offices a voice finally said, "Hello?"

The woman said, "Are yew the Game Warden?"

He said, "Yes."

She said, "Ah finally got the right person. Could yawl gimme some suggestions for a child's birthday party?"

Becker the butcher went to the local bank and said to the Vice President, "I can't meet my note for $10,000 by next Monday. You'll have to give me an extension."

"Sorry," said the banker, "you'll have to get it up by Monday."

"Were you ever in the meat business?" asked Becker. The banker said, "No."

The butcher said, "Well, by Monday you will be."

"Why doesn't your uncle go on the wagon?"

"He would if he could find one with a bar."

Fletcher had a little too much to drink at a party. He went up to the hostess and said, "Pardon me, but does a lemon have feathers?"

She said, "Don't be ridiculous. Of course not."

The drunk said, "In that case, I just squeezed your canary into my drink."

Two brave firemen pulled a drunk out of the burning bed. They screamed at him, "You idiot. This'll teach you not to smoke in bed."

"Who was smoking?" said the drunk. "This darn bed was on fire when I got in!"

"Is it true, Tumulty doesn't like to drink?"

"That's right, it's just something to do while he gets drunk."

Croxall was known as the country club lush. One day at the club bar he was regaling members with his trip to Africa, "There I was on safari, in the jungle, hundreds of miles away from civilization. We had run out of food and whiskey, our throats were parched with thirst . . ."

One of the members said, "But, wasn't there any water?"

"Water? Who could think of cleanliness at a time like this?"

"My cousin Shaun is no ordinary drunk."

"What d'ya mean?"

"I mean, he donated his body to science and he's just preserving it in alcohol till they use it."

When a person goes on a diet, the first thing he loses is his temper.

MIDDLE AGE
That's when you come out of the shower
and you're glad the mirror's all steamed up.

A nurse picked up the phone and said, "Dr. Averbach's office."

A woman said, "Is this really Doctor Averbach's office?"

"Yes, do you wish to speak to the doctor?"

"Er ... no, I guess not. I just found this phone number on a matchbook cover in my husband's coat."

Rosen lost $800 at the poker table and immediately had a heart attack and died. Out of respect for the deceased, the other players continued the rest of the evening standing up. When the game was over, they debated as to how to tell the widow.

"Don't worry," said Lieb. "I'll tell her."

He went to the apartment and knocked at the door. The widow opened it. Lieb said, "Your husband lost $800 playing poker."

Mrs. Rosen screamed, "Lost $800? He should drop dead!"

Lieb said, "He did."

Leach went into a pet shop and said to the owner, "The parrot you sold me stutters. What causes that?"

The owner shook his head and replied, "S-S-S-Search m-m-m-me."

The salesman and his wife arrived in Palm Springs on a combined business and pleasure trip. He ordered the biggest and most expensive dinner in the hotel. His wife made some fast calculations. "Norman," she warned, "that adds up to about three thousand calories."

"So what?" he answered, "I'll put them on my expense account."

The doctor decided to put Mrs. McIntyre on a diet.

"You can have three lettuce leaves," he said, "one piece of dry toast, a glass of orange juice and a tomato."

"Very well," said the woman. "Do I take them before or after meals?"

A yokel nudged the sword swallower at a circus side show and urged that he give a demonstration of his skill. The sword swallower obligingly picked up a handful of nails and needles and gulped them down.

"Hold on there," protested the yokel. "Them wasn't swords."

"I know," said the sword swallower, "but I'm on a diet."

There's one thing to be said for a diet—it certainly improves the appetite.

"Waiter, you've got your thumb on the fish," said the angry diner to the man serving his meal.

" 'Course I have sir," said the waiter. "I don't want it to fall on the floor again."

"Why is it," asked Henri of his stout friend, "that fat people are always good natured?"

"We have to be," said the other, "we can neither fight nor run."

Gribben was enormously overweight. "Don't you ever exercise?" asked a friend.

"I believe in getting plenty of exercise," replied the fat man. "Immediately after waking. I say to myself, 'Ready, now. Up. Down. Down!' And after three strenuous minutes I tell myself, 'O.K. boy. Now we'll try the other eyelid.' "

Abundantly stout Blackburn was advised by his physician to take up golf. A few weeks later he asked the doctor to recommend some other form of exercise.

"In heaven's name, why?" demanded the M.D. "Golf is the finest game in the world!"

"Maybe so," replied the corpulent patient. "But it's not

for me. If I put the ball where I can see it, I can't hit it. And if I put it where I can hit it I can't see it ..."

> Mary had a little lamb
> Some lobster and some prunes
> A glass of milk,
> A piece of pie
> And then some macaroons.

> It made the stupid waiters groan
> To see her order so
> And when they carried Mary out
> Her face was white as snow.

Dieting is the penalty you pay for going over the feed limit.

OBESITY
Surplus gone to waist

Why couldn't the witch eat witch's pie?
Because she was on the witch watchers diet.

"You know what my diet's done for me?"
"Yes, it's made you a bore—you never talk about anything else."

Did you hear about the doctor in Beverly Hills who specializes in weight reduction?
He refers to his patients who worry about their poundage as "my hippo-chondriacs."

Doctor Whitfield has tried for years to persuade his patient Atwater to do something about his being overweight.

One day Atwater asked the medic if he could recommend something to stop him sleeping with his mouth open.

"Of course," said the M.D. "It's your old problem—you must get your weight down."

"My weight?" protested the fat man. "What's my weight got to do with it?"

"Everything! Your skin is now so tight that every time you close your eyes your mouth opens!"

The fattest woman Dr. Risser ever had seen waddled into his office one afternoon and demanded an examination. The physician absentmindedly said, "Okay, open your mouth, please, and say 'moo.' "

Nothing you put in a banana split is as fattening as a spoon.

Doctor: How is your wife getting along with her reducing diet?
Husband: Fine. She disappeared last week.

> A dieting colleen named Flynn,
> Reduced until she was thin.
>> She's no more, I'm afraid,
>> For she sipped lemonade.
> And slipped through the straw and fell in.

Spindly-legged George Bernard Shaw was an avowed vegetarian. He was once accosted by movie director Alfred Hitchcock, who was quite blimpish. Hitch said, "To look at you, G.B., one would really think there was a famine in England."

"To look at you," retorted Shaw, "one would think you had caused it."

What would you call the masseuse at a reducing salon? A blubber rubber!

"I'm having such a tough time dieting."

"What's the big deal? My uncle wakes up every morning and for breakfast he has a dozen eggs, ten pieces of bacon, eight rolls, three stacks of pancakes, two pots of coffee and his weight hasn't changed in twenty years."

"How much does he weigh?"

"Six hundred pounds."

Did you hear about the brand-new diet?

You're allowed to eat whatever you want but you must eat every meal with fat, naked people.

Then there's the new diet pill that doesn't suppress your appetite—it poisons your food.

"Is your wife serious about her diet?"

"Oh, yes. With my wife, weighing is a religious experience. She steps on the scales and utters, 'Oh, my God!' "

A starving man approached a clergyman. "I haven't eaten in over a week."

"The Lord will provide," said the cleric and walked away.

The poor man stopped a politician with the same complaint. "It will be better next year," said the pol and walked away.

In desperation the man stopped an economist and said, "I haven't eaten in over a week."

"Hmmm," said the economist, "and how does this compare with the same period last year?"

The toughest part of a diet isn't watching what you eat—it's watching what everyone else eats.

There was a thin lady named Lena
Who bought a new vacuum cleaner,
But she got in the way
Of its suction one day
And since then, no one has seen her.

Travel broadens you—especially that rich foreign food you eat.

"I just hate the holidays. You're forced to eat so much food."

"For Thanksgiving I'm going on the Southern Belle diet—well, shut mah mouth."

Mrs. Gorman wanted to open a savings account so the bank clerk asked her if she was married. She said, "No, I'm a widow."

"What is your occupation?"

"I am a waitress in a cafe," she replied.

"What did your husband do before he died?"

"He just dropped his can of beer and fell over on the kitchen floor!"

Cora confided to her close friend, "My cooking left my husband cold."

"He divorced you?"

"No," she replied, "he died."

A bum walked up to a big fat woman and said, "Lady, I ain't had anything to eat for three days."

She said, "I wish I had your willpower."

CANNIBAL
That's a guy who loves his
fellow man—with gravy.

A tribe of cannibals put the missionary in a big pot to cook. He said to the chief, "In this day and age how can you still believe in cannibalism?"

The chief said, "Look, I'm an Oxford man—but tradition is tradition."

"An Oxford man—and you speak perfect English. But ... but ... you still eat your fellow man?"

The chief said, "Sure, but now I use a knife and fork."

Lieutenant Berry got a pass for his wife and daughter to visit him at the camp. The two went around to the side gate, which was the shortest route to his headquarters.

But a sentry stopped them. "Sorry, but you'll have to go in through the front gate," he said. "I've got orders, nobody is allowed to pass through here."

"But we're the Berrys," protested the mother.

"Lady, I don't care if you're the cat's pajamas—you can't go through this gate."

Never put off until tomorrow what you can buy today— there will probably be a higher tax on it tomorrow.

A man knocked on the door of the Martinez home. "Can I help you?" asked Martinez.

"Well, I've got good news and bad news, sir."

"What is it?"

"The good news is: you've won the state lottery and a total of three million dollars."

"Oh, fantastic!"

"The bad news is: My name is Jones and I'm from the Internal Revenue Service."

"Alma, how was your date last night with that widower?"

"Awful. He's so cheap he learned Braille so he could read in the dark."

Molly the widow went out with stingy old MacGregor. After a dull evening she said to him, "I'd like to invite you in for a nightcap, but I know you're anxious to get home to your money."

During a riverboat excursion, the weather turned cold and rainy and the passengers huddled together for warmth. The boat captain shouted down to the crew's quarters, "Is there a macintosh down there large enough to keep three ladies warm?"

"No," came the booming answer, "but there's a MacPherson who'd like to try."

A redneck walked into a post office and up on the bulletin board he saw a leaflet that said: MAN WANTED FOR ROBBERY IN MONTANA. The redneck said, "Shucks, if that job was only in Texas ah'd take it."

How would you describe a redneck intellectual?
A guy who doesn't move his lips when he reads.

Did you hear about the redneck who was a bed wetter?
He went to Ku Klux Klan meetings in rubber sheets.

No horse can go as fast as the money you put on it.

A redneck was having a drink in a saloon. His buddy rushed in and said, "Hey, Billy Bob, ah think somebody's stealin' yore pickup."

"Did yew try to stop 'em?"

"Naw, he was too fast," said Slats. "But ah got the license plate number!"

Charlotte got on a crowded bus and held tightly to a strap. Solomon seated in front of her started to rise, whereupon she pushed him back into his seat. "Please don't get up for me," she said. "I'm a liberated woman, and I can stand."

Solomon tried again and again, and the woman refused to let him up each time. Finally, Solomon said, "Look lady, you gotta let me up. I've already gone ten blocks past my stop!"

Burkhardt, a traveling salesman, checked into a motel, opened the Gideon Bible and read the notes on the front page: "If you are sick, read Psalm 18; if you are troubled about your family, read Psalm 45; if you are lonely, read Psalm 92."

The salesman was lonely so he opened to Psalm 92 and read it. When he was through, Burkhardt noticed on the bottom of the page somebody had written, "If you're still lonely, call 682-4379 and ask for Gloria."

You know you've reached middle age when you're sitting home on Saturday night and the telephone rings and you hope it isn't for you.

A sixty-year-old banker met a friend of his at the country club and said, "Cory, I'm nuts about this young girl. You know I'm sixty. Do you think I'd have a better chance marrying her if I tell her I'm fifty?"

His friend said, "I think you'll have a better chance if you tell her you're eighty."

SIGN IN AUTO REPAIR SHOP
We Do Precision Guesswork

Pritchard stood behind O'Donnell while he was in a card game and started to give advice.

"Don't play the jack," said Pritchard. "Play the queen."
O'Donnell did as advised, and won.

Pritchard again whispered to him, "Not the four. The seven."

Once again O'Donnell did as told and won.

Finally O'Donnell got a hand that puzzled him and he whispered to the kibitzer, "Should I play the five or the nine?"

"I'm glad you asked me," said Pritchard, " 'cause I was gonna ask you—what game are you playing?"

Petty and Ralston were coming out of a church after the sermon. "Listen," said Petty, "the word is hallelujah—not Hialeah."

Two horse betters were talking about their luck.

"An extraordinary thing happened to me a few years ago," said one of them. "It was the seventh day of the seventh month, and my daughter was seven years old that day. We lived in a house numbered seven, and I arrived at the race track seven minutes past seven."

"I suppose you backed the seventh horse on the card."

"I certainly did."

"And it won."

"No. It came in seventh."

Did you hear about the old lady who thought her horse was sure to win the Irish Derby because the bookie told her it would start at twenty to one and the race didn't begin until a quarter past?

Paul Revere approached a farmhouse on his famous midnight ride and shouted, "Is your husband home?"

"Yes," replied the woman inside.

"Tell him to get his musket! The Redcoats are coming!"

Revere galloped on to the next farm. "Is your husband at home?"

"He's asleep, Paul!" she replied.

"Tell him to get his clothes. The Minute Men are meeting in the village square. The British are coming!"

Horse and rider galloped on to another house. "Is your husband home?" shouted Revere.

"He's gone to New Amsterdam," answered the pretty blonde from the bedroom window. "He won't be back for a week!"

"Whoa-a-a!"

Did you hear about the guy who had a weird accident?

He fell asleep smoking in bed, burnt a hole in his water bed and drowned.

Now that the Surgeon General has declared war on smoking, the manufacturers are trying to come up with gimmicks to help people quit. They've got one out now . . . it's a cigarette music box. You press a button, a cigarette pops up and the box plays, "Nearer My God to Thee."

Policeman: Did you get the license number of the car that knocked you down, ma'am?

Woman: No, but the driver was wearing a beige three-piece linen suit lined with pink crepe, and she had on a periwinkle hat trimmed with red roses.

A careful driver approached a railroad; he stopped, looked, and listened. All he heard was the car behind him crashing into his gas tank.

Matson arrived at his parked car and found this note on the windshield:

"I'm terribly sorry I hit your car. I'll never do it again."

Two beer drinking buddies were telling riddles. A short-stop, an umpire, three sports writers, an auto mechanic and a preacher were in the maternity waiting room. Whose wife had the triplets?

The mechanic. They always go over the estimate.

The most common cause of car sickness is still the sticker price on the window.

At a big auto show, a dealer saw Weiss consult the price tag on a new model, smile happily, and summon his wife. The dealer explained, "That price tag, you must realize, covers only the federal, state, county, and city taxes. The price of the car is additional."

Wife: I had to leave the car. There was water in the carburetor.
Husband: Where is it now?
Wife: In the lake.

Did you hear about the parking attendant who got a winter job as a cloakroom attendant?

After only a week at his new job, he had dented 17 over-coats.

Some people believe that the English don't have a sense of humor. That's not true. An Englishman laughs at a joke three times: Once when he hears it. Once when it's explained to him. And once when he understands it.

A Cherokee Indian chief in Oklahoma was lying beside the road with his ear to the ground. A fellow walked up close and overheard the chief say, "White man! Lincoln Continental! Minnesota license plate. Smoke big cigar.

Blonde woman sit beside him. Smoke cigarette. Drink fire-water."

"That's fantastic!" exclaimed the man. "Can you tell all that just by putting your ear to the ground?"

"No!" cried the chief. "They run over me."

After Henry Ford had made a fortune in the automobile industry, he decided to return to the land his father had emigrated from, County Cork, Ireland. When Ford arrived in Cork he was greeted by a committee of public-minded citizens who were trying to raise money for a new hospital. Ford immediately took out his checkbook and wrote a check for $5,000.

The next day in the newspaper there appeared a full page ad thanking Mr. Ford for his generous contribution of $50,000.

Later that day, the Committee reappeared at Ford's door and apologized, stating that the error was the typesetter's fault and that they would print a retraction in the following day's paper. "I think I have a better idea," said Ford.

He told the Committee he would give them a check for the additional $45,000 if they would allow him to have something inscribed over the main entrance. Naturally, the committee agreed. Ford made out the check and chose a scripture from Matthew which can be seen today: "I came among you as a stranger and you took me in."

Humor Bibliography

This is a partial list culled from the more than two thousand volumes of joke collections on my book shelves. It represents a lifetime of work and a labor of love.

The list includes mostly hardcover books. However, many of them have been reprinted in paperback.

The focus is on collections that will be of assistance to speakers, writers, editors, executives, politicians, clergymen and others who must appear before the public.

Adams, Joey. *From Gags to Riches.* New York: Frederick Fell, Inc., 1946.

Adams, Joey. *Joey Adams Joke Book.* New York: Frederick Fell, Inc., 1952.

Adams, Joey. *Joey Adams Joke Dictionary.* New York: Citadel, 1962.

Adams, Joey. *Encyclopedia of Humor.* New York: Bobbs-Merrill Co., 1968.

Adams, Joey. *Son of Encyclopedia of Humor.* New York: Bobbs-Merrill Co., 1970.

Adler, Larry. *Jokes and How to Tell Them.* New York: Doubleday, 1963.

Asimov, Isaac. *Treasury of Humor.* New York: Houghton-Mifflin, 1971.

Blakely, James "Doc". *Handbook of Wit & Pungent Humor.* Houston: Rich Publishing, 1980.

Blakely, James "Doc". *Push Button Wit.* Houston: Rich Publishing, 1986.

Braude, Jacob M. *The Treasury of Wit and Humor.* Englewood Cliffs: Prentice-Hall, 1964.

Braude, Jacob M. *Handbook of Humor for All Occasions.* Englewood Cliffs: Prentice-Hall, 1958.

Braude, Jacob M. *Speaker's Encyclopedia of Stories.* Englewood Cliffs: Prentice-Hall.

Cerf, Bennett. Fifteen Joke Collections. New York: Doubleday, 1944–1972.

Copeland, Lewis & Faye. *10,000 Jokes, Toasts & Stories.* New York: Garden City, 1939.

Dickson, Paul. *Jokes.* New York: Delacorte Press, 1984.

Esar, Evan. *The Humor of Humor.* New York: Bramhall House, 1953.

Esar, Evan. *20,000 Quips and Quotes.* New York: Doubleday, 1968.

Esar, Evan. *The Comic Encyclopedia.* New York: Doubleday, 1978.

Esar, Evan. *Esar's Comic Dictionary.* New York: Doubleday, 1983.

Fechtner, Leopold. *5,000 One & Two Liners for Any & Every occasion.* West Nyack: Parker Pub., 1973.

Fechtner, Leopold. *Encyclopedia of Ad-libs, Insults & Wisecracks.* West Nyack: Parker Publishing, 1977.

Fechtner, Leopold. *Galaxy of Funny Gags, Puns, Quips & Putdowns.* West Nyack: Parker Publishing, 1980.

Gerler, William R. *Executives Treasury of Humor For Every Occasion.* West Nyack: Parker, 1965.

Helizer, Melvin. *Comedy Techniques for Writers & Performers.* Athens, OH: Lawhead Press, 1984.

Helizer, Melvin. *Comedy Writing Techniques.* Cincinnati: Writer's Digest, 1987.

Humes, James C. *Instant Eloquence.* New York: Harper & Row, 1973.

Humes, James C. *Podium Humor.* New York: Harper & Row, 1975.

Jessel, George. *You Too Can Make A Speech*. New York: Grayson, 1956.

Jessel, George. *The Toastmaster General's Guide To Successful Public Speaking*. New York: Hawthorn Books, 1969.

Kearney, Paul W. *Toasts and Anecdotes*. New York: Grosset & Dunlap, 1923.

Lieberman, Gerald F. *3,500 Good Jokes for Speakers*. New York: Doubleday, 1975.

Lieberman, Gerald F. *3,500 Good Quotes for Speakers*. New York: Doubleday, 1983.

McManus, Ed & Bill Nichols. *We're Roasting Harry Tuesday Night*. Englewood Cliffs: Prentice-Hall, 1984.

Orben, Robert. *Complete Comedian's Encyclopedia Volumes I, II, III, IV, V and VI*. New York: Lou Tannen, 1951–1959.

Orben, Robert. *Encyclopedia of One-Liner Comedy*. New York: Doubleday, 1966.

Orben, Robert. *2100 Laughs for All Occasions*. New York: Doubleday, 1982.

Perret, Gene. *How to Write and Sell Humor*. Cincinnati: Writer's Digest, 1982.

Perret, Gene. *How to Hold Your Audience with Humor*. Cincinnati: Writer's Digest, 1984.

Prochnow, Herbert V. & Son. *A Dictionary of Wit, Wisdom & Satire*. New York: Harper & Row.

Prochnow, Herbert V. & Son. *New Guide for Toastmasters and Speakers*. New York: Prentice-Hall, 1956.

Prochnow, Herbert V. & Son. *The Public Speaker's Treasure Chest*. New York: Harper & Row, 1977.

Rosten, Leo. *Giant Book of Laughter*. New York: Crown, 1985.

Saks, Sol. *The Craft of Comedy Writing*. Cincinnati: Writer's Digest, 1985.

Wilde, Larry. See: Books By Author.

Woods, Ralph L. *The Modern Handbook of Humor*. New York: McGraw-Hill, 1967.

The San Francisco Public Library houses the most complete collection of comedy in the United States, possibly the world. It contains more than 17,000 volumes of wit and humor by the greatest humorists who ever lived.

Attorney Nat Schmulowitz, a respected member of the California legal profession and gifted storyteller, founded the collection in 1947.

An entire wing has been set aside to store what has become known to humor historians and lovers of comedy as **the Schmulowitz Collection of Wit And Humor**.